Patterns of Magnificence

TRADITION AND REINVENTION
IN GREEK WOMEN'S COSTUME

Dedicated to the memory of Koula Lemos

Patterns of Magnificence

TRADITION AND REINVENTION IN GREEK WOMEN'S COSTUME

EDITOR:

Ioanna Papantoniou

ESSAYS:

Nadia Macha-Bizoumi

Sofia Pantouvaki

Ioanna Papantoniou

Maria Passa-Kotsou

Myrsini Pichou

Xenia Politou

Angeliki Roumelioti

This book was published to accompany the exhibition

Patterns of Magnificence
TRADITION AND REINVENTION IN GREEK WOMEN'S COSTUME

held initially at the Hellenic Centre, London (4 February – 2 March 2014), and subsequently at the Teloglion Foundation of Art, Thessaloniki (March – June 2014), the Foundation of the Hellenic World, Athens (July – September 2014), and the Leventis Municipal Museum, Nicosia (October 2014 – January 2015).

The exhibition, its associated events and production of this catalogue were sponsored by George and Natasha Lemos and Dinos and Calliope Caroussis in memory of their mother, Koula Lemos.

Proceeds from the sale of the catalogue in the UK will be retained by the Hellenic Centre to further its cultural objectives. Proceeds of the sale of the catalogue in Greece and Cyprus will be donated to various charities on Chios.

EDITORIAL ADVISOR: Natasha Lemos

CATALOGUE COORDINATOR: Maria Papadopoulou

CATALOGUE ENTRY EDITORS: Maria Papadopoulou, Angeliki Roumelioti

TEXT EDITOR (ENGLISH EDITION): Alexandra Pel

TEXT EDITOR (GREEK EDITION): Georgia M. Panselina

TRANSLATOR: Timothy Cullen

INDEX: Theophilos Tsifos

PHOTOGRAPHY: Yannis Patrikianos, Costas Vergas

SECRETARIAL ASSISTANCE: Asimina Valasaki

GRAPHIC DESIGN: Thymios Presvytis, Thodoris Anagnostopoulos

IMAGE EDITOR: Ilias Perdikoulis

LAYOUT: Dimitra Triantafyllou, Angeliki Houndi

PRODUCTION: Peak Publishing

PRINTING: Baxas S.A.

ISBN: 978-0-9525518-3-6

First published in Great Britain by:
The Hellenic Centre
16-18 Paddington Street
London W1U 5AS

Front and back cover:
Mórkos, a long, sleeveless, pleated dress from Skopelos, Sporades. Early 20th century (cat. no. 17)

Contents

Preface

This exhibition, the largest and most representative of one of the great costume traditions in Europe ever to have been mounted in London, has been the work of many hands since it was first proposed by one of us, Natasha, as a tribute to the memory of our mother, Koula Lemos.

Ioanna Papantoniou, of the Peloponnesian Folklore Foundation, eagerly replied to the proposal, and through her work and that of her collaborators, Maria Papadopoulou and Angeliki Roumelioti, turned the riches of the Foundation's collection into what the visitor can now enjoy. Mrs Papantoniou's deep and unparalleled knowledge of the subject has created a thematic structure which is truly impressive and original. This structure has been given physical form through the imaginative design of Stamatis Zannos.

Angelos Delivorrias and his colleagues at the Benaki Museum generously agreed to lend items to supplement the Peloponnesian Folklore Foundation's collection, as did Eleni Tsaldari and her colleagues at the Lyceum Club of Greek Women.

On the suggestion of Edmée Leventis, Ian Jenkins and Judy Rudoe at the British Museum enthusiastically responded to the exhibition by arranging for the display of textiles from the Museum's own collections in the Parthenon Galleries and to take part in public events at the Museum and the Hellenic Centre. We hope that this will be the beginning of a long chapter of cultural cooperation between the Hellenic Centre and that great institution.

Maria Lemos and her colleagues Bianca Fincham and Lucy Hemelryk at Rainbowwave worked tirelessly to connect the exhibition with the world of contemporary fashion. The noted designer Marios Schwab generously agreed to promote the exhibition, and we hope that the concurrence of the exhibition with London Fashion Week will stimulate the designers of today to reinterpret the riches of the past. Thanks are also due to Stavroula Saloutsi, editor-in-chief of *Blue*, the magazine of Aegean Airlines, and to her associates Panos Kokkinis and Xenia Georgiadou for including an article about the exhibition in their magazine.

Thymios Presvytis, the designer of the catalogue, Timothy Cullen, the translator, and Georgia Panselina and Alexandra Pel, the text editors, spared no effort to meet deadlines. To them and to the authors of the catalogue essays, we are very grateful, as we are to all those who have agreed to give the evening talks which will accompany the exhibition.

Finally, at the Hellenic Centre we thank Agatha Kalisperas and her staff, Maria Kalli, Evangelia Roussou, Kay Stavrinou and Christina Vagioti, as well as the Chairman of the Executive Board, Sophie Kydoniefs, for their work in smoothing the organisational path for the success of the exhibition.

The Hellenic Centre was a cause dear to the heart of Koula Lemos. In hosting for the benefit of the public in Britain an exhibition of the hidden riches of one of the great and individual traditions of Greece, the Hellenic Centre is surely fulfilling the aims conceived 20 years ago by the other founding members and by her.

George and Natasha Lemos
Dinos and Calliope Caroussis

Welcome Note

It is with great pleasure that we welcome this unique exhibition of traditional Greek costumes to the Hellenic Centre. The rich collection of crafted fabrics and embroidered costumes with accompanying jewellery and accessories is truly magnificent.

The catalogue, a breathtaking record of the exhibition, is enhanced by contributions written by specialists in the field.

We are happy that the exhibition is taking place in 2014, which is also the Hellenic Centre's 20th anniversary.

The aim of the Centre is to bring together Greek and Greek-Cypriot excellence in a programme of diverse cultural events promoting Hellenism to the wider community. Over the years thousands of people have attended our lectures, concerts, exhibitions and Greek language courses and they have joined us at social evenings celebrating Greek customs and traditions.

This exhibition, in memory of our beloved founder member, Koula Lemos, was made possible by her family. We are deeply grateful to them.

Agatha Kalisperas
Director of the Hellenic Centre

Introduction

The 'Vassilios Papantoniou' Peloponnesian Folklore Foundation is this year celebrating its 40th anniversary and London's Hellenic Centre its 20th. On the occasion of these anniversaries the Peloponnesian Folklore Foundation is presenting the exhibition *Patterns of Magnificence: Tradition and Reinvention in Greek Women's Costume* at the Hellenic Centre.

In the development of women's local costume in Greece during the 18th century, one can discern survivals of garment forms from a period for which we have very little relevant information. These forms were the basis of what was to follow in the mid-19th century, when, with the Romantic Movement, local costume came to assume a fixed appearance in Greece, Western Europe and elsewhere.

Two types of garment form the starting point: the dress from Kassos and Karpathos, a three-metre-long dress with a fold which recalls the *kolpos* of the Ionic chiton; and the loose, pleated dress from Crete, which seems to have taken its shape in Italy during the Renaissance. The two representative examples of these dresses, which belong to the Benaki Museum, Athens, are those which constitute the foundation of the costumes of the Aegean.

A series of chemises introduces the dalmatic, a garment from which other Greek costumes were derived. The dalmatic, owing to its simple line, was supplemented all over the Balkans by a series of garments worn one over the other during the long period of Ottoman rule. Thus, over the basic Byzantine rural dress, as this evolved after the Roman period, we find various urban outer garments: the *anderí*, the *kavádi*, the kaftan, the *doulamás* (*dolama*), the *sayás*, the *pirpirí* and the *dzoumbés* (*cübbe*).

Two examples of court dress, the costume introduced by Queen Amalia in 1837 and that subsequently created by Queen Olga in 1867, influenced both urban and rural costumes in Greece.

Ioanna Papantoniou
Costume Designer and Historian of Dress
President, Peloponnesian Folklore Foundation

The Development of Costume in the Sphere of Influence of Greek Civilisation*

Ioanna Papantoniou

PREHISTORY

We do not know when or why human beings first started covering their bodies. One thing we do know is that they started wearing skins, literally entering into an animal's skin, probably to identify with it. We also know that the memory of this practice lingered on in the ritual vestments of the Mediterranean peoples at least until the dawn of the historical era. Anthropologists have observed that in tribes which for one reason or another have lagged behind in the march of evolution, the people first 'adorned' themselves and then 'dressed' themselves (fig. 1).

In Greece, the oldest textile was found at Lefkandi on Euboea (1000 BC): it is actually a complete funerary garment of linen, in plain weave with a band of more complex weave. It is now in the National Archaeological Museum in Athens, together with other cloth fragments from Lefkandi. In the Bronze Age in the Eastern Mediterranean, and also at similar stages of cultural development in the Scandinavian countries and elsewhere in Northern Europe and among many primitive peoples in our own time, fringed garments occupy an important position: probably the fringes are the natural loose ends of narrow or broad strips of cloth.

In the 2nd millennium BC, on Thera (Santorini), on Crete and among the Mycenaeans in mainland Greece, we find fringed lengths of cloth that were wrapped in many different ways around the body, especially round the hips, probably as accessories to the more formal women's ensembles. It may be that those fringed garments were the distinctive wear of certain social groups, if they were not ritual vestments. It is difficult to arrive at a firm conclusion without oral testimony to back up the evidence of the garment itself (fig. 2).

The looms of that period must have been vertical ones with weights (warp-weighted looms). Weights of this kind have been found at Archanes on Crete (Sakellarakis 1994: 62). They probably coexisted with ground-looms, which had certainly been in use in Egypt for some time, as attested by a wall painting from the tomb of Khnumhotep (XIIth Dynasty, 2000-1785 BC) in the Metropolitan Museum of Art, New York. Warp-weighted vertical looms probably evolved out of the need to tauten the vertical threads (the warp) of makeshift contrivances for the 'weaving' of grass sacks, like the structure drawn by Clark Wissler in 1917 (Broudy 1979: 15) (fig. 4).

Fig. 1. The magical identification of man and beast still survives, as at the Arkoudes (Bears) Festival, held annually on 6 January at Volakas, near Drama.
Peloponnesian Folklore Foundation Photographic Archive, Nafplio

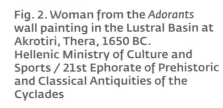

Fig. 2. Woman from the *Adorants* wall painting in the Lustral Basin at Akrotiri, Thera, 1650 BC.
Hellenic Ministry of Culture and Sports / 21st Ephorate of Prehistoric and Classical Antiquities of the Cyclades

Fig. 3. *The Contemplative Athena*, votive relief of Parian marble, *c.* 460 BC. The goddess, barefooted, wears an Attic peplos.
Photo: Socrates Mavromatis. Acropolis Museum, Athens.

The plasticity and liveliness of pictorial representations of clothes, hairstyles, jewellery and art in general in the prehistoric Aegean come as a pleasant surprise after the solemn and weighty art of the Assyrians, Babylonians and other Asian peoples or the delicate rigidity of Egyptian wall paintings.

Following the eruption of the Thera volcano (*c.* 1500 BC) and the decline in the power of Crete, the Mycenaean civilisation spread from the Peloponnese to the whole Mediterranean basin. There ensued a troubled period consequent upon a series of disasters (11th century BC), a period described by M. A. Edey (Edey 1979) as the 'Dark Ages' since very little is known about it. Two hundred years later, there emerged first the Archaic period with its splendid costumes and then the incomparable Classical period, which was of greater importance for human development.

Fig. 4. A primitive loom used by native Americans to make straw bags. Straw can only be woven to a height of a few centimetres on this kind of loom.
From C. Wissler, *The American Indian*, 1917

THE HISTORICAL ERA: GEOMETRIC, ARCHAIC AND CLASSICAL PERIODS

The information about clothing to be gleaned from Homer refers to the Geometric period. However, the changes occurring after that were limited, so to us they look like variations on the same theme. That is only natural, given that all ancient Greek garments were made of rectangular pieces of cloth differing only in the material, the decoration and the way they were fitted onto the body.

Homer, then, informs us that the usual men's garment was the chiton or tunic: made of white linen, it was worn loose and was sewn only at the shoulders and the sides. Over the chiton, which was a *periblema* (a garment covering the body), men wore the *pharos*, which was an *epiblema* (an outer garment, cloak or mantle). The linen *pharos* was also white. Another kind of cloak was the woollen *chlaina*, which was dark in colour: the archons or chief magistrates wore a dark red or purplish-red *chlaina*. In winter, the *chlaina* was also used as a coverlet. The chiton worn by farm workers, labourers and soldiers was always short. Long chitons were worn by priests and charioteers, and more generally by the Ionians, who for that reason were known as *helkechitones* ('trailing the tunic').

Women wore a long, coloured peplos of fine wool with a variety of ornament (*poikilos peplos*). It was a sleeveless garment with a girdle round the waist and was sometimes called *heanos*, meaning a garment suitable for many uses (*Ιστορία του Ελληνικού Έθνους*, II 1971: 456) (figs 5–5a).

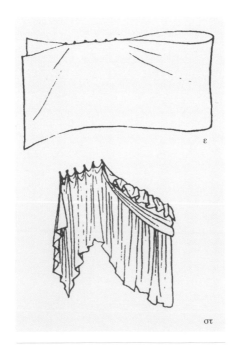

Figs 5–5a. Patterns: (α-β) peplos, (γ-δ) chiton and (ε-στ) women's himation.
Peloponnesian Folklore Foundation Archive, Nafplio

In the Archaic period women's dress underwent a change, and the peplos or Doric chiton was replaced by the Ionic chiton. Herodotos explains why in a well-known story (*Hist*. V.87-88). After the Athenians were routed on Aegina in 568 BC, the sole survivor made his way back to Athens with news of the disaster. The women, on learning of the slaughter of their menfolk, stabbed him to death with the fibulae (brooches resembling safety pins) that were used to fasten the peplos. From that time on the Athenian archons banned the peplos. A similar use of the fibulae is to be seen in the tragedy *Hecuba*, where the women put out the eyes of the Thracian king Polymestor with the pins from their peploi. Oedipus, too, gouged his eyes out with the pins from Jocasta's peplos (fig. 3).

An outer garment worn by both men and women was the himation, a rectangle of woven wool that covered the shoulders in various ways: this we know from representations of it, mostly on amphorae and other vases. Another, worn by young men, was the chlamys, a sort of cloak fastened with a clasp on the right shoulder. It was usually worn by horsemen, who let it stream out behind them (Karamanos: 145). The *ampechonon* was a medium-sized shawl or wrap, and the *ampechonion* a slightly smaller and lighter version of it: they were worn by women, apparently draped over the back, folded in two lengthwise, covering part of the shoulders and held in place by a girdle round the waist, so that it partly covered part of the hips at left and right. Yet another type of wrap was the *ampechone*, a small woollen shawl of shaggy weave worn by women and some effeminate young men. Identifying a particular garment depicted in ancient art as an *ampechone* is usually speculative at best.

In the Classical period, from the late 6th century BC onwards, the Doric style of dress came back into fashion, that is to say a chiton worn as a peplos, often over the Ionic chiton, which was now of finer material, with its numerous folds gathered together into a sort of oval bib at the front. Men, too, wore a short woollen Doric chiton with the himation. Peasants usually wore the *exomis*, a short woollen chiton which left one shoulder uncovered.

Spartan men went on wearing a short woollen chiton, the *tribon*, as before, while their womenfolk wore the *phainomeris*, a short woollen peplos like an *exomis* but open on one side. The peplos at this time was much wider and often made of linen. The peplos or Doric chiton and the Ionic chiton were woven on a warp-weighted loom (*histos*) by one woman or two together, who wove standing up, passing the shuttle with the weft to and fro between them. The huge rectangular cloth produced by such a loom (about the shape and size of a double sheet) was draped over the body. The cloth was fastened over the shoulders, either with a large fibula on each shoulder (the peplos) or with several smaller pins at intervals from the shoulder to the elbow (the chiton), with the pin pointing forward in each case.

If the piece of cloth was too long, it was tied round the waist to stop it trailing on the ground. The surplus was then allowed to hang down on the outside, forming a fold called the *apoptygma* (overfall), or pulled up in front to form a sort of blouson, the *kolpos*. Often there was a *kolpos* as well as an *apoptygma*. This freely flowing garment was often fastened at the shoulders with straps in various arrangements: the *maschalister*, for example, was a continuous band that was crossed over at the back and passed under the armpits so as to form 'sleeves'. Thus the 'sleeved chiton' came into existence.

HELLENISTIC AND ALEXANDRIAN PERIODS

Clothing remained very much unchanged in the Hellenistic and Alexandrian periods (323-30 BC), especially for the masses. On women's chitons the girdle was placed higher, just below the bosom. Widespread use was made of cotton from India and also of silk (*bombykine metaxe*), presumably from China. Imported luxury garments were all the rage with rich ladies. The gossamer silks from Kos were particularly highly regarded. In fact, women dressed so showily in those days that they looked almost like courtesans. The gold decorative motifs woven into luxury fabrics are echoed in the gorgeous gold jewellery of this period: magnificent specimens of the goldsmith's art are to be seen today in museums.

The 'sleeved chitons' of this period have real rather than schematic sleeves, following the example of 'barbarian' sleeved garments (fig. 6).

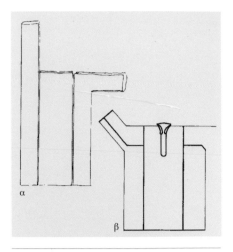

Fig. 6. (a) Sleeved chiton of the Hellenistic period, (β) the Greek chemise that later developed from the sleeved chiton.
Peloponnesian Folklore Foundation Archive, Nafplio

The sleeve, especially a close-fitting sleeve, presents one of the great problems in cutting and sewing. Centuries were to elapse before dressmakers and tailors grasped the principle of inserting the sleeve into a shaped armhole. What is difficult is to shape the armpit in such a way as to allow the arm to move freely from the shoulder. If the garment is close-fitting, attaching the sleeve to the bodice calls for the hand of a true master tailor. The problem was dealt with at different times in different ways, which are not always apparent in works of art: to obtain the desired result, a painter or sculptor will leave out anything he finds artistically difficult, because he is either unable or unwilling to tackle it. The same is true of men's trousers, where the crotch presents the same difficulty as the armhole. Both problems vary according to the elasticity of the fabric, so it was often easier to make a knitted sleeve or trouser leg.

At first the sleeves were set well away from the shoulders. As they gradually came closer to the body, so the problems multiplied. One solution is to have a wide sleeve with a square armhole (what is now called a 'peasant armhole' in Greece), which can be made easier to handle by adding a square insertion (known in Greek villages as a *vathráki*) in the armpit. Another, possibly derived from the Ionic chiton, is to follow the pattern of Anatolian shirts with a rectangular piece of cloth inserted as an oversleeve, and even odder is its Cypriot variation with a long triangular gusset at the shoulder. Yet another is to have very long, tapering sleeves fastened at the wrist, which push the length of the sleeve up towards the shoulder, forming horizontal folds.

Fine-textured pleated chitons, which had to be fitted onto a small yoke to hold the garment in position on the shoulders, probably evolved into the loose, flowing dresses of the Greek Islands and the Renaissance. Any different impression can be attributed, in my opinion, to the use of newer thick cotton materials and brocades.

EARLY CHRISTIAN PERIOD – BYZANTINE COSTUME

A major turning point in the history of Greek clothing was the foundation of the Eastern Roman Empire, where a new, different, brilliant civilisation, that of Byzantium, gradually developed. Although clothes were still based on Roman clothing, they now incorporated elements borrowed from the civilisations of Asia and acquired a distinctive look that left its mark on the history of Oriental dress. The most important item borrowed by the Byzantines, and by other Europeans too, was the outer garment, similar in cut to the clothing they had always worn but open all down the front. Until then, the outer garment's place had been taken by large stoles, shawls and cloaks (the chlamys, himation, toga, *stola* and *chlaina*). Various different types of garment were stirred together in the melting pot of Byzantine costume, and from them the distinctive costumes of the Mediterranean and Balkan peoples evolved.

The Byzantine emperors deliberately allowed themselves to be influenced by the East, especially Persia. Their subjects created a provincial Byzantine style of their own which was later to win over the Ottoman conquerors, who captured Constantinople in 1453 but were themselves overcome by the dazzling Byzantine civilisation. François Boucher (Boucher 1967) explains the significance of the establishment of a Christian empire in western Asia, where the civilisation of Sassanid Persia was steadily gaining ground.

Medieval writings contain countless references to Byzantine clothing, and there are also thousands of kilometres of wall paintings in churches depicting saints and layfolk wearing the costumes generally called Byzantine. Further pictorial information is provided by illuminations in manuscripts and other written works and by portable icons, which often feature benefactors as well as saints. This material covers a very long period of time and a huge geographical area, the area of Byzantine cultural influence. The foreign-sounding words used with reference to clothing in Byzantine writings are very hard to identify with the garments depicted in Byzantine art. It seems to me that the basis is to be found in Roman costume, which was adopted not only throughout the geographical sphere of influence of Greek civilisation, which Alexander the Great had extended eastwards, but also further north, west and south. During this period a clearer picture of the costume situation began to emerge.

The garment forms that became standard in the Early Christian period in the Mediterranean countries were based on the dalmatic, which evolved from the Roman *tunica*. The dalmatic is made up from more than one piece of cloth. The main part is a long, rectangular strip of cloth hanging down at the back and front, with an opening in the centre for the head. Separate sleeves are sewn on to this, and additional gussets are let into the side seams, making it possible for the garment to fit the shape of the body to some extent without narrowing at the hem. This garment lived on for many centuries in Greek local costumes and was known as a *poukámiso* (which nowadays means 'shirt').

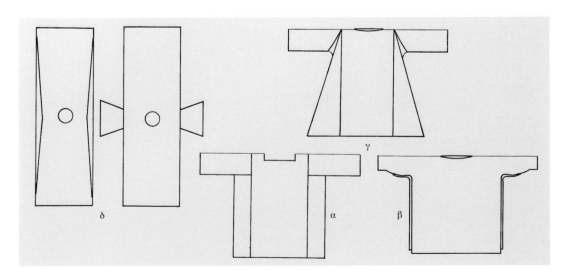

Fig. 7. Patterns: (α, γ) dalmatic, (β) *tunica*, (δ) tunic with sleeves added. Peloponnesian Folklore Foundation Archive, Nafplio

Fig. 8. Coptic tunic as it comes off the loom.
Museum of Greek Folk Art, Athens

Naturally enough, the dalmatic evolved differently in the East and the West. In the East, owing to a stagnation in the evolution of costume design that followed the Turkish conquest, garments based on the dalmatic and *tunica* became almost 'set in stone' and were confused with Oriental garments of similar cut, so much so that today it is hard to tell which garment is derived from which (fig. 7).

Complete garments from the Early Christian period have been found in tombs at Antinoe, Faiyûm and Aswan in Egypt, and in other places where the dry climate has preserved the fabric in good condition. Although they have not been precisely dated, they are thought to cover the period between the dawn of Christianity and the early 7th century AD. Their decorative designs, at first Hellenistic in style, were fused as time went on with local forms and later with Oriental motifs. They were called 'Coptic' garments after the Copts (Egyptian Christians), who had a long tradition of weaving and were fanatical guardians of their national traditions. Although Greek was the official language of Egypt in the Roman as well as the Alexandrian period, the Copts used the Greek alphabet – with the addition of some symbols from the Egyptian demotic script – to write their own language. Many of the Copts later embraced Islam to avoid the heavy taxation imposed by the Byzantine administration, but many remained faithful to Christianity and are now one of the most important social groupings in Egypt, with much cultural good work to their credit. An excellent study of the Coptic garments and fabrics in the Museum of Greek Folk Art (formerly the National Museum of Decorative Arts) in Athens was published by Anna Apostolaki in 1932. The most recent work on Coptic fabrics is an *édition de luxe* by Marie-Hélène Rutschowscaya (Rutschowscaya 1990).

The method of weaving the *tunicae* found in Coptic tombs is of some interest (fig. 8). They were woven on a frame-loom, in the shape of a cross, according to Vernardakis (Vernardakis 1906), because of the symbolism of the Cross. Dorothy K. Burnham (Burnham 1973) describes how one of the tunics in the Royal Ontario Museum in Toronto was woven. The width of the warp is twice the length of the tunic when folded in two on the shoulders. The weaver wove from the bottom up: first one sleeve, then the body, leaving an opening for the neck, and finally the other sleeve. The side seams are formed by tying the loose threads of the warp. The decorative designs on these garments, if not woven in, have been woven on a frame and are sewn on or inserted at the desired points. Many of the *tunicae* of this period are made of more than one piece of material and make use of the coloured selvages (ochre, blue and red) for decorative purposes.

Garments similar to the ones found in Coptic tombs are very vividly depicted in the mosaics of the 3rd and 4th centuries AD in the Roman villa of Casale at Piazza Armerina in Sicily (Capizzi & Galati 1989). The clothes pictured in the mosaics supply a wealth of information about the costume of the period: men's loincloths, tunics of all types, chitons, mantles, women's drawers and brassieres, breeches. The mosaics also show clearly how the legs were protected by criss-cross thongs (*fasciae*), as well as the kinds of shoes that were worn and a great deal of jewellery.

In the famous mosaics in the Church of San Vitale, Ravenna, it is easy to see the relationship between the clothes depicted at Piazza Armerina and the sumptuous garments worn at the court of Justinian and Theodora. Here again, the principal garment is the tunic with its *segmenta* and *clavi*. The laymen to the right of Justinian, the emperor himself and the two men to the right of Theodora wear an outer garment, the chlamys (*sagum*) with square *tabulae*[1] on the breast. The *tabulae*, purple or gold-embroidered or made of costly brocade, are the distinctive marks of the aristocrat's chlamys. They were probably placed in this position to cover the seams of the internal pockets. Nowadays, we find the same kind of pockets in shepherds' capes. The mantle is fastened by a fibula on the right shoulder.

The churchmen wear wide-sleeved tunics or dalmatics, white and possibly made of linen. The middle section of these garments is outlined by the dark selvages on the right and left. The dalmatic, which eventually superseded the Roman *tunica*, was originally long and made up of several sections sewn together. The women's dresses and the three women's mantles shown in the mosaics are of brocade. The hem of Theodora's white robe is decorated with gold-embroidered columns, and a single column can be seen on Justinian's hem. All are wearing *epimaníkia* (overcuffs). Cloth-of-gold silks from the East were imported in large quantities in Justinian's reign. It was a period of sweeping change. The narrow horizontal loom established itself as the standard type. Garments became closer-fitting, because the imported fabrics were narrower. From this time on we find references to garments with strange names, probably derived from the material they were made of: *kavádia*, *skaramángia*, *tzitzákia* and *devitísia*, for example. Some of them were very heavy and are described as *solinotá* (tubular) or *syrmatéina* (made with wire).[2] The *tambári*, the *granátsa* and the very long-sleeved *lapatsás* were over garments of 'barbarian' origin, which generally superseded the earlier outer garments.

Thus, the basic garment for men and women was the tunic, which was gradually transformed into the dalmatic and survived in the local costumes of the Balkans and the Eastern Mediterranean, either as the principal garment or as the basis of more complex ensembles, worn with short or long over garments of various kinds, with one or the other overlapping, depending on the material of which they were made.

The short chemise or smock survived as a farm worker's garment in all the local costumes of Europe. In the Balkan Peninsula – especially in Greece, and more particularly in the whole of the Peloponnese, at Megara and in Macedonia – it was an item of everyday wear, but also formed part of the festive costume until the early 20th century. Elsewhere it remained in use as an undergarment which men tucked into their trousers or wore under a short over garment.

Long chemises were originally made of plain woven material. They were ornamented in the same way as Coptic chemises, that is with decorative stripes (*clavi*), independent decorative motifs (*segmenta*) and square decorative appliqués (*tabulae*) which were embroidered, woven or dyed purple. The long chemise survived as a basic element of all rural women's costumes in the Balkans.

Costumes were rounded off with a cloak of some sort, originally the toga or the *sagum* (familiar in Greece as the chlamys), known by various names. The toga was worn by the Romans in a special way, folded and at the same time wrapped round the body in such a way as to leave the gold-embroidered selvages showing. One important type was the *toga picta et palmata*. All that survived of it in the Byzantine period was the *chrysópaston clavion* ('clavus shot with gold') of the selvages: this was worn as a sash wrapped round the body and was called a *loros* or *lorus*.

The practice of making women's robes very long appears to have influenced the development of the dalmatic, too. Woman wore a girdle round the waist, making a shallow or deep *kolpos*. However, they also wore a chemise, completely loose. The 'short over long' look, strongly insisted upon by the artist Yannis Tsarouchis as a Greek custom, might be achieved by the presence of the *kolpos*; otherwise two chemises would be worn, a short one over a longer one. The short chemise might be sleeveless. This ensemble with two *tunicae* survived in the local costumes of the Eastern Balkans and Russia, and also everywhere in Greece with the variation of having the *tunica* open down the front.

In the interesting garment from Kassos (p. 82) and Karpathos depicted by Otto Magnus von Stackelberg (Stackelberg 1825), we see the shape of the dalmatic coexisting with the *kolpos* of the chiton. In the pattern illustrated here (p. 82) the dotted line marks the line of the internal fold; Stackelberg has depicted it correctly. Dresses of this kind, dating from the early 19th century, can be seen in the Benaki Museum, Athens, and the Victoria and Albert Museum, London. One might even go so far as to compare the overfold on the Kassos garment with the overfold on terracotta statuettes of the Cypro-Archaic and Classical periods from Achna, Cyprus (Caubet 1998). It is my belief that the horizontal pleats on Greek dresses of the modern era are 'fossilised' relics of this very ancient practice (fig. 9).

The practice of overfolding is still in use in Palestine and Syria. For a wedding, the bridal dress is actually hung on the outside of the house from the eaves, about 3-3.5 metres above the ground. The bride inserts herself into the dress from below, holding her arms straight up; the dress is girdled with a cord under the arms; the upper part of the dress is then allowed to hang down and the bride's arms are put into the sleeves. In this way the dress is given a triple fold.

It seems most likely that the early 19th-century dress from Kassos had its origin in Asia Minor, especially when one compares it with miniatures of noble Byzantine families in the founder's *typikon* of the Convent of the Mother of God Bebaia Elpis in Constantinople (14th century), formerly in the Bodleian Library (now in Lincoln College, Oxford). There, the ladies wear clothes of sumptuous materials, with no front opening, with sleeves hanging down to a sharp point and pleats at knee level, exactly as still to be seen today in Palestinian costumes. The men wear a long, close-fitting, cassock-like robe fastened down the front. A garment similar to the ladies' dresses mentioned above, but all white, is depicted clearly in a fresco in the cave church at Agios Sozomenos in Cyprus.

Only in the costumes of Palestine and Syria do we still find long pendant sleeve-points added on separately – often so long that women tie them together behind their backs when working. The practice of tying the sleeves together behind the back is also found on Astypalaia: the sleeve-points of the Astypalaian chemise have specially made cords attached to them, which are tied behind the back to keep the sleeves out of the way.

In mainland Greece, sleeves with triangular inserts are found only in the Argolid, where research has already brought to light a curious resemblance to the old white dresses of Palestine. The similarities in the form and arrangement of decorative designs on the neck opening and hem of a group of chemises from the Argolid and Corinthia, not unlike the ornamentation of Palestinian dresses, may or may not be coincidental. The ubiquity of the Argolic-Corinthian ensemble all over the Peloponnese in the mid-19th century has also been noted by students of the costumes of Attica, Boeotia, Phthiotis, Phokis and Euboea. This is possibly due to a more unified 'Byzantine' rural fashion in mainland Greece. In conservative rural communities, such as the villages in Attica inhabited by

Fig. 9. Terracotta female figurine from Achna, Cyprus, 6th century BC. Musée du Louvre, Paris

Arvanites (Greeks of Albanian descent), outfits of this kind remained in use until the late 19th century and sometimes even the early 20th, whereas in the villages of Lakonia they lay forgotten in trunks and chests. So closely was this Attic costume associated with the Arvanites that in the early 20th century it was known as *arvanítika*.

POST-BYZANTINE AND MODERN PERIODS

Little is known about the development of costume in historically Greek lands in the Post-Byzantine period. Secular and religious art, though plentiful, is stylised and was kept within certain guidelines, and so it adds little to our knowledge of the costumes of that period and certainly does not concern itself with the way the rural population dressed. Consequently, Greek local costumes, most of which belong to the rural areas, have to be studied from an evolutionary point of view in the context of the history of costume in those parts, either from writings in which the references to clothes are obscurely worded, or more often from the descriptions given by foreign travellers in regions that had become part of the Ottoman Empire (Papantoniou 1996a).

Leaving aside the Ottoman 'urban fashion' worn by people engaged in middle-class occupations, all the evidence is that the rural populations went on wearing a Byzantine-type farm worker's garment that altered little over the years, and that mainly in its ornamentation, not in its structural elements. This is quite understandable, considering the isolation of most rural areas.

On the other hand, the places visited by travellers on their way from Europe to the Holy Land or Constantinople did have some contact with the West, and so they were influenced by the European way of dressing, though always some way behind the fashion. In the Aegean Archipelago those European ways, modified always by residual memories of earlier periods and adaptation of the 'alien' styles to local needs and habits, appear to have given rise to a curious fashion idiom for women, while the standard garb for men gradually came to be the universal nautical garment of breeches, probably Moroccan in origin but known by their Celtic name, rendered in Latin as *braccae* and in Greek as *vráka*, which to a Western European was synonymous with trousers (fig. 10).

For men, the above-mentioned peasant costume remained as it had been in the Middle Ages, that is, a pair of breeches with a short, loose smock. Over this they would wear a waistcoat of some kind and a sleeved or sleeveless over garment. The outfit was held in at the waist in various ways. In the north the smock was often tucked into woollen breeches.

The foustanella or short kilt, as worn by the *klephts* and *armatoles* (brigands who joined the struggle for Greek independence in 1821) and celebrated as the Greek 'national costume', was adopted as court wear by King Otto in the mid-19th century. The foustanella has recently been the subject of a lengthy and highly derogatory study

Fig. 10. *The Forty Martyrs*, early 12th-century wall painting from the Church of Agios Nikolaos tis Stegis. Kakopetria, Cyprus

by Ilias Petropoulos. His book, which is definitely worth reading, includes articles on the foustanella by Z. Papantoniou, T. Lappas and A. D. Keramopoulos (fig. 11).

Greek women's local costumes began to lose their distinctive identity owing to the continual importation of the 'latest' Western European fashions – at first by Queens Amalia and Olga, who were not Greek – and also to the continuous contact between small towns and the capital and between villages and the small towns.

From about 1837, when Amalia, the first Queen of Greece, instituted a form of court dress (known as the 'Amalia' costume) modelled on traditional Greek costumes, urban dress started changing in imitation of the new style. The influence of the 'Amalia' costume was felt not only by women in the provincial towns of liberated Greece but also by women throughout the Balkans and as far away as Cyprus.

The industrialisation of Greece in the late 19th century coincided with the reign of Queen Olga, who took the lead in founding vocational training schools for women; and, with the sewing machine taking the country by storm, village women adopted a form of dress including a skirt, polka jacket, apron and kerchief, which is also found, with variations, in all the Mediterranean countries and even beyond (fig. 12).

Nowadays, Greek local costumes have completely disappeared from the villages, except in a very few places, such as Karpathos and Metsovo. They are revived only as stage costumes for dance companies in the villages themselves (organised by local cultural societies, day care centres for the elderly, etc.) or elsewhere (by the Lyceum Club of Greek Women, the Dora Stratou Greek Dance Theatre, etc.) (Papantoniou 1996b).

It may be that the evolution of local costumes will have to be documented from the wardrobes of dance companies. Since the 1960s, dance companies have been creating their own costume designs for dance performances. Their outfits were often composed of authentic items, but often also of copies. Preference was given to bridal and festive costumes, though that was not always possible.

In the late 19th century Greek men and women adopted Western European fashions, though it proved impossible to establish a Greek *haute couture* with corresponding ready-to-wear clothes in spite of the movement pioneered in the 1960s by Yannis Tseklenis. Abroad we find Greeks rising to great heights as fashion designers, including Jean Dessès in France and Yiannis Evangelidis, James Galanos and George Stavropoulos in the United States (figs 13, 14).

In the 1970s we should not forget the 'back to tradition' movement of Nikos and Takis and a number of improvised styles, mostly created by young Greek women who had the courage to combine fashion with traditional-style accessories (the *tagári* [woven shoulder bag], *sigoúni* [long, open, sleeveless embroidered jacket], *tsembéri* [kerchief], *haimaliá* [amulets], etc.) and inset ornaments from the so-called 'Thracian' (but actually Turkish) *tsevrés* (embroidered runner or kerchief).

The unadventurous design of the Greeks' everyday clothes nowadays is in sharp contrast with the design of theatrical costumes. Whether the inspiration is based on tradition (Yorgos Ziakas) or whether it borders on surrealism (Dionyssis Fotopoulos), one does find real inspiration in the theatre, worthy of the creative spirit of the Greeks.

Fig. 11. Urban costume with foustanella that belonged to one of the aides of Ioannis Kapodistrias, the first Governor of Greece. Peloponnesian Folklore Foundation, Nafplio

Fig. 12. Skirt and polka jacket in a Manchester gingham check. Early 20th century. Peloponnesian Folklore Foundation, Nafplio

Fig. 13. 'Tunic' and swimsuit by Yannis Tseklenis from his 'Waves' collection. Athens 1974. Peloponnesian Folklore Foundation, Nafplio

Fig. 14. Dress by Yannis Tseklenis from his 'Insects' collection, worn by Efi Mela at her last fashion show. Athens 1972. Peloponnesian Folklore Foundation, Nafplio

NOTES

1. *Segmenta*, *clavi* and *tabulae* are decorative motifs, either sewn on as appliqués or woven in.

2. Phaidon Koukoules discusses whether these terms refer to the type of garment or the type of fabric: see Phaidon Koukoules (1948), *Βυζαντινῶν βίος και πολιτισμός* [Byzantine life and civilisation], vol. II, Athens, Papazisis Editions, pp. 5-59.

* This essay is a slightly revised version of an article that first appeared in the periodical *Endymatologica* 1, Nafplio, Peloponnesian Folklore Foundation: 17-25.

The Chemise of Greek Women's Local Costumes
(19th – Early 20th Century)

Angeliki Roumelioti

The *poukámiso*, or chemise (*kamísion* [Latin *camisia*]), an essential part of every Greek local costume, is a basic garment worn short by men and long by women, which was in use for many centuries in Europe and other parts of the world. It was worn as an undergarment and was cut in such a way as to facilitate the wearing of outer garments of similar cut.

The chemise of Greek local costumes is morphologically a continuation of the dalmatic (Papantoniou 1978: 8); and the dalmatic (fig. 1) is considered to be an imaginative and elaborate Roman variation of the tunic (*tunica*) (fig. 2) from which most subsequent Eastern and Western garments are derived (Papantoniou 2000: 89). There are two theories concerning the origin of the name 'dalmatic': either that it is derived from Dalmatia, whose inhabitants wore a garment of that kind (Houston 1934: 120-121), or because it was originally made of white Dalmatian wool (Boucher 1967: 166). The dalmatic was introduced by the Romans around the end of the 2nd century AD, initially as a men's garment, and it gradually came to be worn by both sexes (Boucher 1967: 166).

A decisive factor in the development and form of garments is the width of the loom, because it determines the width of the cloth (Burnham 1973: 9). In practice, the *tunica* can be made of a single piece of cloth twice the length of the garment, with an opening for the head at the centre and with two one-piece sleeves sewn on. The dalmatic differs in that it has gussets inserted at the sides, which alter the basic shape of the garment and make it easier to create variations to suit the place and time. The dalmatic went out of fashion around the 5th century, but the same pattern was used by Orthodox priests for some liturgical vestments (Boucher 1967: 166), and the name is still used today to denote Roman Catholic, Lutheran, Anglican and Methodist vestments.

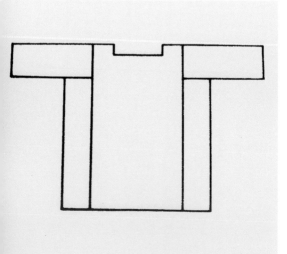

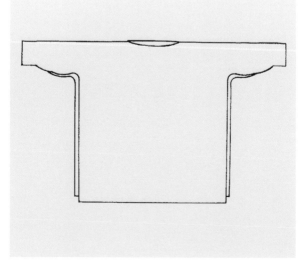

Fig. 1. Pattern of a dalmatic. Peloponnesian Folklore Foundation Archive, Nafplio

Fig. 2. Pattern of a *tunica*. Peloponnesian Folklore Foundation Archive, Nafplio

The Empress Theodosia, wearing a *tunica*. Detail from a tomb wall painting in Antinoopolis. 6th century AD. From Marie-Hélène Rutschowscaya, *Coptic Fabrics*, Éditions Adam Biro, Paris 1990

The women's chemises of Greek local costumes may be white or coloured and consist of a single rectangle of material (the *mána*) covering the front and back, having the full width of the cloth woven on the loom – never more than 45-50 centimetres – and with no seam at the shoulders. At the sides, to make the garment wider and more comfortable for walking, triangular gussets were inserted below the armpits: these were called *langhiólia* (from the Latin *lanciola*, a small lance: see Kyriakidou-Nestoros 1983: 89) or *ladzoúlia*, *lóxes*, *loxária*, *klínghia*, etc. They may be sleeved or sleeveless, with a round neckline, with or without a collar, and there was a vertical opening in the bib, sometimes reaching right down to the abdomen to leave ample room for the head to go through and to facilitate breastfeeding. At the neck, if it was not left open, the chemise was fastened with a string or with one or more buttons. Some of the chemises in a bride's dowry were left uncut at the neck, and the neck opening was cut only when the garment was about to be used. The embroidered bib that used to be a feature of some chemises was replaced by a sewn-on facing of printed fabric or velvet (Papantoniou 1978: 10). Particular attention was paid both to the construction of the sleeve, to ensure that it permitted free movement, and to its ornamentation. The sleeve reached down to the wrist and was wide or very wide, with or without gathers at the shoulder. The sleeve was inserted into a square armhole (a 'peasant armhole'), sometimes with the addition of a square insertion (*vathráki*) of the same or a different material in the armpit, to give greater freedom of movement (Papantoniou 2000: 83).

Chemises are divided into two main categories: those that go with village costumes, worn almost exclusively by the women of the rural population (see the costumes of the Karagouna, p. 102, of Attica, p. 104, and of Corinthia, p. 108), and those that go with urban costumes, which are the preserve of urban women (see the costumes of Ioannina, pp. 186-193, and Pyrgos, p. 80, and the 'Amalia' costume, p. 206).

In the country, every family processed the raw materials – cotton, silk, linen, hemp, wool and so on – and made the cloth it needed, depending on what was produced locally. In the period under consideration, factory-made fabrics for chemises were extremely rare. When the village women were not working in the fields, they were busy weaving, knitting and embroidering. In addition to their everyday needs, they had to set to work from an early age on their dowry and presents for their future in-laws. They made the chemises by themselves from start to finish, often undertaking the whole process from gathering the raw material, preparing it, making it into cloth and dyeing it, to sewing the garment and adding the ornamentation. In places where the necessary raw material was not produced, they took on seasonal work, for which they could be paid in kind (Papantoniou 1976: 421). As time went on, however, it became more usual for them to buy the yarn ready-made and carry out the rest of the process themselves.

The stage of preparing the yarn before weaving was important because proper processing ensured not only better quality but also greater durability, in times when clothes were worn until they could be worn no longer. The method of processing the yarn depended on the kind of raw material and local custom. For making cotton chemises, to ensure that the warp would be durable and sufficiently elastic and would not 'ball up' or get jammed in the reed, most village women subjected the yarn to a process called *káïsma*, which involved soaking it in a mash of flour mixed with hot water. This was done twice, with the warp left soaking in the mash overnight each time (Papantoniou 1976: 421). In Macedonia and Thrace, olive oil and soap were added to the mixture. When the warp was dry, they prepared it for installing in the loom and threading through the shafts and the reed. Once the cloth had been woven they bleached it by immersing it in animal manure and then, after washing and beating it, leaving it out in the sun to dry out and bleach a bit more. At Krokos, in the prefecture of Kozani, they bleached it by soaking it in lime wash, beating it and then drying it in the sun: they did this eight times, and finally it was washed with soap in warm water (Kyriakidou-Nestoros 1983: 72-73).

Long experience and careful attention were needed again for the dyeing of yarns and fabrics. The technique was passed on from generation to generation, and usually the most experienced of the older women taught the younger ones. At first only vegetable dyes were used, but in the course of time they were superseded by synthetic aniline dyes bought from pedlars, which were much easier to use. The range of colours obtainable from vegetable dyes was limited, and the colours chosen in different parts of the country depended on the leaves, roots, fruits, nuts, barks and plant fibres available locally. Another factor which made a great difference to the hues yielded by the dyes was the quality of the water. The vegetable dyes most commonly used for different shades of red included madder (*Rubia tinctorum*), onion skins, kermes scale insects (*Coccus ilicis*), *arkélia* (seaweed plant) and the stigmas of the crocus. The main sources of black dye were the bark of the alder (*Alnus glutinosa*) and the leaves of the ash (*Fraxinus ornus*), oak (*Quercus* spp.) and sumach or smoke-tree (*Rhus coriaria*). Yellow dyes came mainly from walnut and almond leaves and the bark of crab-apple trees, and brown mainly from walnut husks (Kyriakidou-Nestoros 1983: 68-72). The yarns were done up into loose skeins in such a way as to leave the ends accessible. The dyeing was done in a cauldron of boiling water. Since it was generally believed that anything with a sour or acid taste makes the colours fast and stops them from fading, after being dyed the yarns were plunged into a prepared solution, most commonly of alum in water. They were then rinsed thoroughly, and as soon as they were dry they were ready for use (Loukopoulos 1927: 14-15).

The chemises of town costumes differed considerably in their materials and in the way they were constructed. They were usually made of linen, silk or a linen-silk fabric, woven in specialised workshops. Townswomen therefore had the option of buying only the cloth or the whole chemise ready-made, sewn and decorated in the appropriate way. The workshops supplied fabrics and chemises to the pedlars, who sold them on to customers. Since the pattern of the chemise was standardised, no distinction could be drawn from the cut of the garment: high social status or wealth was indicated solely by the quality of the decoration and materials.

Angeliki Hatzimichali observed that on the islands the chemise was always made of linen or silk. On the mainland, however – except in Epiros (see the costumes of Ioannina, pp. 186-193) and at Trikeri, Thessaly (see the chemises and costume of Trikeri, pp. 94-101, 132) – it was made of a thick cotton material. She also noted that in the costumes with the *sigoúni* as their outer garment (see, for example, the chemises from Corinthia, pp. 108-115, and Attica, p. 104) the chemise was again of thick cotton, sleeveless and lavishly embroidered with geometric designs. In the costumes that included an outer garment of the *kavádi*, *anderí*, *sayás* or *kaplamás* type (see, for example, the costumes of Stefanoviki and Pyrgos, pp. 166, 180, and the *sayás* from Pylaia, p. 168), the chemise was long and made of cotton, linen or silk of varying quality, with long, wide sleeves edged with embroidery and lace. In the costumes with a *foustáni* (see, for example, the costumes of Psara, p. 144, Astypalaia, p. 138, and Skyros, p. 134), the chemises varied in quality: they were made of thick or thin cotton, linen or silk and were wide, with long sleeves. In the costumes with baggy breeches, which had embroidered decoration on the legs, the chemise was short enough to leave the embroidery visible (Hatzimichali 1978 I: 16-17).

The patterns for all chemises were carefully worked out so that no material would be left over when the sewing was done, not only for reasons of economy but also to save the dressmaker time and trouble (Burnham 1973: 3). The cut of the chemise had nothing to do with the girl's figure: her approximate measurements were calculated according to the age she would be when she wore it. The width of the chemise never varied, even when the wearer was pregnant. If it needed to be widened, gussets were inserted between the *langhiólia*: these were long, narrow pieces of material, wider in the middle and tapering to a point at one end. In this way, extra width was added where it was needed (around the middle) without increasing the circumference of the hem (Tsangalas 1993: 230). If it was ever necessary to shorten a chemise, a horizontal pleat was added, usually at waist height.

According to their cut, chemises can be divided into the following categories (Papantoniou 1978: 8-9):

a) Chemises in which the width is gathered at the neck. They are derived from Renaissance undergarments and are found on the Ionian Islands and Crete, and in other Balkan countries too. Chemises of this type are also depicted in 19th-century prints of costumes from the Peloponnese (Mani and Arcadia), though the garments themselves have not survived (fig. 3).

b) Chemises in two parts, with a seam at the waist, of the same or a different material, close-fitting on the torso and with a gathered skirt. Here again, traces of Renaissance influence can be seen. These chemises are found in the Dodecanese, on Chios and on Skopelos and Skyros in the Sporades (see, for example, the chemise pattern from Astypalaia, p. 138).

c) Chemises with the *langhióli* prolonged to form a long sleeve. Here, there are traces of Turkish influence (fig. 4).

d) Chemises in which the *langhiólia* start from the armpit or the sleeve hole. The majority of the chemises in Greece are of this type (see, for example, the chemises from Corinthia, pp. 108-115, and of the Karagouna, p. 102).

All the chemises in the first category, those of Astypalaia, Nisyros and Tilos in the second category and those that are influenced by the chemise of the foustanella costume (Aitolo-Akarnania, Souli, the Sarakatsani) have long, very wide sleeves gathered at the shoulders (Papantoniou 1978: 9). A typical case in point is the bridal costume of Astypalaia: because the sleeves of the chemise were so very wide, when the bride wanted to put on the *manikotó* (sleeved) dress, she would tie them round at the wrists with a cord sewn onto the sleeves. Since their weight and width made it difficult for her to get dressed, she kept the sleeves raised and fastened behind her back with the same cord (Tarsouli 1947 II: 330; see also 'The Women's Costume of Astypalaia' by Maria Passa-Kotsou in this catalogue, pp. 38-47, and fig. 6, p. 42). In the Argolid

Fig. 3. Hand-coloured print of a Greek country woman wearing a chemise gathered at the neck. Inscribed: 'Paysanne Grecque (Morée). Turquie, Egypte, Grèce etc., 19, Moine Imp.r.de Noyers, 47, Paris, A. Portier'. From a series of albums of hand-coloured prints of costumes from all over the world, published by the Musée Cosmopolite. Paris, 1850-1863. Peloponnesian Folklore Foundation, Nafplio

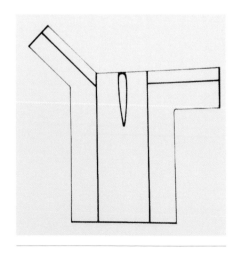

Fig. 4. Pattern for a chemise from Soufli, Thrace. Peloponnesian Folklore Foundation Archive, Nafplio

Fig. 5. A *skolopendráto* chemise from Astypalaia, Dodecanese. *c.* 1870. Peloponnesian Folklore Foundation, Nafplio

and Corinthia one sometimes finds a type of chemise with a triangular gusset in the inner seam of the sleeve (see the two examples on pp. 108, 114). Ioanna Papantoniou pointed out the similarity of these garments to the chemises of Palestinian costumes, with regard both to the triangles in the sleeves and the arrangement of the decoration (Papantoniou 2000: 126-127).

The decoration on a chemise was embroidered, woven-in or sewn on and depended on the girl's artistic taste and her family's financial circumstances. It was an area of fierce competition, because a costume was one way of showing off. To save time, materials and labour, the decoration was usually confined to the sleeves, hem, neckline and neck opening, the areas that were not covered by other parts of the costume or accessories. The designs bore traces of classical, Byzantine, Italian and Turkish influences. The motifs were drawn from the animal and plant kingdoms, everyday objects and scenes and occupations of the local people. For example, the *skolopendráta* chemise of Astypalaia (fig. 5) took its name from the strips of embroidery resembling centipedes (*Scolopendra* is a genus of centipede) on the sleeves; and the *mastrapás* is a design found on the bridal chemise of Attica which resembles a jug of a shape used in the East (see the Attic chemise, p. 104). Very often the name of a design was derived from the name of the woman who first used it or the village where that particular 'fashion' originated. The motifs and colours of the designs were so standardised that the place of origin – and sometimes the actual village – is immediately recognisable. So, although the designs on the hems of chemises from Vocha and Perachora, Corinthia (fig. 6), closely resemble those on the chemises from Boeotia (fig. 7), in spite of the great distance between them their place of origin is still instantly identifiable: the difference lies in the stitch, which in Corinthia is a mixture of stitches with the single stitch predominant (Papantoniou 1976: 422). According to the oral testimony of Ioanna Papantoniou, this difference is due to the fact that women from Corinthia, who worked in the cotton fields of the Argolid or Boeotia, copied the designs from local chemises and then adapted them to their own technique.

There were two kinds of embroidery on the chemises: the *xombliastá* (drawn embroidery) and the *graftá* (literally, 'written', i.e. counted-stitch embroidery). When doing *xombliastá*, by counting the stitches the embroiderer can create repeated patterns, as on the chemises from the Peloponnese and the linen chemises from Trikeri (see pp. 94-101). In the *graftá*, on the other hand, the designs are drawn freehand on the cloth, in ink, and are embroidered without counting, usually with the aid of a frame, as on the silk chemises for formal wear from Trikeri and Skyros (see p. 134). However, some embroidery had to be done by a professional embroideress, because they were too difficult for a non-specialist (see the chemise from Attica, p. 104).

In Attica, all the girls learnt to embroider from an early age. Helped by their mother or grandmother, they would embroider the chemises for their dowry in the appropriate way for the purpose for which they would be used. The embroideries on the hem of the bridal and festive chemises would be done by a specialist embroideress (*maístra*), of which there would be at least one in every village in Attica (Hatzimichali 1978 I: 31). According to Linda Welters (Welters 1988: 57), however, the *maístres* were only in the big villages, and the best of them all were to be found in Koropi. They had a special talent for embroidery and made it their full-time occupation, to support their families financially. Potential customers would select the one with the best reputation and hire her to embroider the hems. The embroideries, mostly *graftá*, were done in multicoloured silks, with red predominating. Angeliki Hatzimichali observed that it is extremely time-consuming work: in fact, if the embroidery round the hem was particularly high, three *maístres* were needed to complete the decoration. The first one drew the design on the cloth; the second embroidered the outlines using dark thread and stem-stitch and filled in the blue and green parts; and the third embroidered all the rest with the help of assistants (Hatzimichali 1978 I: 31). The filling stitches most commonly used were Gobelin and stem filling (Welters 1988: 57). Maria Michail-Dede (Michail-Dede 1981: 50, 52) noted that sometimes the *maístra* embroidered the whole hem herself, while sometimes she merely drew the design and made a start on the embroidery, leaving the girl to do all the rest under her guidance. The hem embroideries show remarkable variety (Welters 1988: 78) with regard to:

a) the height: the higher the embroidery, the richer the bride.

b) the colours – of which there may be as many as 22-24 (Welters 1988: 69) – and shades of colour, after the darker vegetable dyes were superseded by brighter aniline dyes.

c) the designs, which changed from generation to generation.

d) local peculiarities: every village might have its own variations.

e) the designer's inspiration.

Girls from poor families, who could not afford to have the hem embroidered by a *maístra*, could either borrow their bridal chemise from a relative or wear their mother's *foúndi* (bridal chemise) or embroider the hem themselves, in which case it would have very little height (Welters 1988: 49). However, if the girl became engaged to a wealthy man, her fiancé would pay for the work; then the *maístra me ta chrysá* would take the

Fig. 6. Bridal chemise from Perachora, Corinthia. Early 20th century. Peloponnesian Folklore Foundation, Nafplio

Fig. 7. Bridal chemise from Tanagra, Boeotia. Early 20th century. Peloponnesian Folklore Foundation, Nafplio

chemise, with its hem already embroidered with silk thread, and embroider over all or part of it with real gold thread (fig. 8), using a technique similar to that of the Byzantine imperial and ecclesiastical *chrysosklavariká* embroideries (Hatzimichali 1978 I: 32).

Woven-in decoration is found mainly in northern Greece, sometimes with brocaded designs and sometimes with stripes. The stripes might be coloured either at the selvages (*kinária*) or at the ends, creating a pattern by the way the parts of the chemise were sewn together (fig. 9); or else they formed a chequered pattern in blue and ochre. Stripes of the same colour as the background were quite common: they stood out because of either the weave or the quality of the material (see, for example, the chemise of the costume from Psara, p. 144).

A special case is the bridal chemise from the area of Drymos, Macedonia, known as the *poukámiso me ta sarídia* (fig. 10). The visible parts – the hem, the lower part of the sleeves and the borders of the neck opening – were made of wool and cotton or wool and silk, in orange-red, crimson or bright red, and were decorated with woven-in stripes and designs. The rest was of pale blue *aladzás* with blue stripes, either straight or criss-crossed.

Lastly, the sewn-on decorative elements used on women's chemises included braid, ribbons, lace, *bibíles*, sequins and beads, among many others (see, for example, the chemises from Skyros, p. 134, and Skopelos, p. 120).

One of the few types of chemise adorned with jewellery was the bridal chemise (the *pekámiso*) of Kastelorizo (see the costume on p. 154). Its neck opening, reaching from the neck to the stomach, was fastened with four or six gold or silver-gilt *voúkles* (buckles),

Fig. 8. Hem of a bridal chemise from a costume from Kifissia, Attica, that belonged to the Koutsos family. Early 20th century. Peloponnesian Folklore Foundation, Nafplio

each with a hole in the middle and a pin to fasten it to the cloth; these were decorated with floral motifs, often enamelled.

Throughout Greece, chemises fall into one of three categories – everyday, festive and bridal – according to their ornamentation and the materials they were made of. There were also differences indicating the wearer's age and marital status. For example, at Trikeri (see the chemises and costume from Trikeri, pp. 94-101, 132) there was a wide range of different chemises to be worn on the appropriate occasions. The best ones were made of fine silk (*sképi* or *olóskepo*) in white or scarlet (*áliko*). The white kind was worn by young girls, including those engaged to be married, and the scarlet by brides. The white ones were embroidered with silk thread and gold metal thread, the scarlet with gold thread. The typical design of the hem embroidery on the formal chemises consisted of *korvétia*, upright or aslant, a *korvéti* being a branch with twigs, leaves and flowers, and *petropoúlia* (birds) perched on the tips. The formal chemises made of *sképi*, worn by married women, were dark red (*arkiláto*) or a medium red (*kremizí*). The formal chemise worn by women married to men who travelled was a blackish green with silver embroidery. Widows generally wore a very dark, almost black chemise with no embroidery. The chemises worn with the everyday costume were the *liná* (linen) or *déftera* (second-rate), which were white or blue, woven with a linen warp and silk of inferior quality for the weft. They were decorated with *xombliastá* in multicoloured silk. Young women wore both colours, older women only the blue.

Differentiations of dress really started with marriage: the best chemise was worn on formal occasions, while for everyday use a woman would wear chemises with less elaborate decoration or of less costly material. These distinctions gave rise to the differentiation between formal and everyday wear. The festive and bridal chemises can be told apart from the everyday garments by the quality of the fabric, the neatness of the sewing and the number of embroideries. A newly married woman usually started wearing every day the chemises that until her wedding she had worn only on festive occasions. Five to ten years after marriage she stopped wearing the formal chemise and wore instead the best of the second-rate garments. Widows often wore plain, all-white chemises as a sign of mourning. No distinction was made between winter and summer wear.

Fig. 9. Bridal chemise from Soufli, Thrace.
Early 20th century.
Peloponnesian Folklore Foundation, Nafplio

Fig. 10. *Poukámiso me ta sarídia*, bridal chemise from Drymos, Thessaloniki.
Early 20th century.
Peloponnesian Folklore Foundation, Nafplio

Depending on their financial circumstances, women usually made most of their chemises for their dowry. Rich girls and poor had in their dowries enough clothes to last them all their life; quite often, in fact, they had more than they needed and passed on the ones they never wore to be added to their daughters' dowries. Most of the chemises were made for the owners' youth and middle age, and relatively few for their old age. We know from personal statements and dowry contracts that a rich bride in Attica generally had in her dowry twenty-four embroidered chemises and at least six unembroidered ones for everyday wear and old age (Hatzimichali 1978 I: 29), while a bride in the Soufli area was endowed with sixty chemises, more than anywhere else in Greece (Hatzimichali 1983 II: 329). Brides in the Argolid and Corinthia took five or six with them in their dowries and gave the bridal chemise to two other brides in accordance with local custom. Another very widespread custom was to keep the bridal chemise for the 'longest journey', which explains why so many bridal chemises have not survived.

All chemises – both those intended for the owner's use and those kept in readiness for a daughter's dowry – were looked after with the greatest care, for every woman was very well aware of the value of her clothes. The women of Trikeri used to starch their formal chemises with rice water and dry them in the sun, partly to prevent their becoming shiny when ironed and partly to stiffen the material (Hatzimichali 1931: 159). On Skopelos the *anetoráli*, or bridal chemise (see the costume from Skopelos, p. 120), was made of pure silk and had long, wide sleeves. Each sleeve had a broad band of ornamentation – dense gold-thread embroidery – at the end and embroidered stars at intervals, embellished with gold *trémouses* and tiny pearls; since the gold thread turned black, the chemises were kept wrapped in soft white paper (Delitsikou-Papachristou: 5-58).

The chemise was a very important part of all Greek local costumes – so important, in fact, that in spite of the sweeping changes in modes of dress following the invasion of West European fashions, it went on being worn in simplified form under the novel garments before finally being abandoned after World War II (Papantoniou 1978: 9).

The Women's Costume of Astypalaia

Maria Passa-Kotsou

Astypalaia (Astypálaia, Astypaliá, Astropaliá, Stampalia), an isolated island in the Aegean lying between the Cyclades and the Dodecanese (to which it belongs administratively), is shaped like a butterfly with open wings. An isthmus divides the island into two parts, the western, with the main town, or Hora, with its Venetian castle, and the eastern. Its area is 97 sq. km; its highest point is the hill of Profitis Ilias, at 506 m; and the length of its much-indented coastline is 110 km. In the 2011 census its year-round population was recorded as 1310, and the local economy now depends mainly on tourism.

Immediately after World War II, when it had already been decided that the Dodecanese, under Italian occupation since 1912, should be united with Greece, the artist and writer Athina Tarsouli visited the island (Tarsouli 1996). At that time, Astypalaia had about 1000 inhabitants, who eked out a living from sponge-fishing, from the few patches of cultivable land and from the remittances sent home by islanders who had been driven to emigrate by poverty and the Italian occupation. While roaming through the alleyways of the town, she met the 80-year-old Maria Patinioti, who was wearing 'the local costume with all its brightly coloured trimmings [...], a *kaliaráto* chemise [see below], a fiery red dress, a cap with gold embroidery of the double-headed eagle, an orange kerchief, etc.' (Tarsouli 1996: 14); Tarsouli made a sketch of the costume (fig. 1). She tells us a good deal about the local costumes, often illustrated with her own drawings, and remarked on the willingness of the local women to open up their clothes chests and show her the costumes worn by their mothers and grandmothers, which they themselves no longer wore except on special occasions. She classified the costumes into four distinct types,[1] following the example of Marica Montesanto, who had been to Astypalaia in the early 1930s (Montesanto: 1930?).

Fig. 1. **This may have been the same Maria Patinioti that Athina Tarsouli had drawn some years earlier. She is wearing an everyday *misó* costume with a sewn-on apron and the sleeves of the chemise turned up.**
Photo: Maria Chrousaki, 1950.
Benaki Museum Photographic Archive, Athens

Montesanto visited the island at a time of rampant Italian nationalism. She had her own reasons for going there, however, as her family, originally from Piacenza, had emigrated to Astypalaia around the end of the 14th century; later, probably after 1540, they moved to Cephalonia after Astypalaia had been captured by the Ottomans. She made

good use of the known facts about the Venetian presence on the island and also the local oral tradition connecting one particular type of costume with the local (Venetian) gentry.

In 1207, following the Fourth Crusade and the dismemberment of the Byzantine Empire by the Latins, Marco Sanudo, Duke of Naxos, ceded the island to the Venetian nobleman Giovanni I Querini. For over 300 years, expect for a brief reversion to Byzantine rule (1269-1310), Astypalaia served as an advanced defensive outpost of La Serenissima. According to the local historical tradition, early in the 15th century Giovanni IV Querini installed 'the descendants of the 12 "brides"' (fig. 2) in the residential quarter of the walled town and 'granted them the right to wear the *chrysomandiláta* [or *chrysomándilo*, described below] and the privilege of leading the "classic" dance in the forecourt of the church' (Montesanto 1930?: 15-16).[2]

In 1537, Hayreddin Barbarossa captured Astypalaia for the Ottomans. With its safe natural harbours, it gave them a good base for controlling the seaways of the eastern Aegean, especially the route from Alexandria to Constantinople, which were favourite targets for pirates. In fact, as one historian noted, 'The Astypalaians' everyday contact with piracy accustomed them to the idea of living on the fruits of plunder. There were periods when the town developed into an unbridled centre of local piracy, with no distinction being drawn between the pirates' nationalities or the ships' flags.' (Patellis 2001: 86).

Fig. 3. *Chrysomándilo* with *skolopendráto* chemise. The *chrysés vétses* (stockings) are missing. The *veloúdo* and the *chrysí fellí* (mules) were kindly lent by Themelina Haralambopoulou-Kastanou. Late 19th century. Lyceum Club of Greek Women, Athens

The costumes of Astypalaia known to us today date from the late Turkish period, that is, the late 18th century and, more especially, the early 19th. On the Aegean Islands, local costumes gradually fell into disuse, embroidery techniques were forgotten, and the products of domestic handicrafts changed hands and found their way into collections (Wace & Laurence 1914; French 2009). On Astypalaia it has taken rather longer for this to happen, so visitors and scholars have been able to see and admire the local costume, which survived here and there on the island and was known for its unusual and distinctive character. The archaeologist and collector Alan J. B. Wace[3] remarked that – judging mainly by the women's costumes – the embroideries of Astypalaia were 'of a peculiarly complicated character' (Wace & Laurence 1914); Montesanto pointed out that the local culture

Fig. 2. A group of 12 women wearing the *chrysomandiláto* costume in the Church of St George in the castle. It is conjectured that they are descendants of the 12 'brides' (*ninfe* or *spose*) installed by Giovanni IV Querini in the castle of Astypalaia. From Marica Montesanto, *L'Isola dei Gigli (Stampalia)*, 1930. Benaki Museum, Athens

developed between the two poles of Byzantium and Venice (Montesanto 1930?: 25); Tarsouli described the costume as 'a blend of Byzantine and Venetian tastes' (Tarsouli 1996: 35); and Papantoniou as 'a rarity among costumes', in which 'some Northern European elements survive' (Papantoniou 1991: 135). Typologically, it is an ensemble 'with a dress', that is, a dress 'of the Western, old (Renaissance) type' (Hatzimichali 1978: 15; Papantoniou 1978: 13).

The four variants of the women's costume are the *chrysomándilo*, the *skléta*, the *ieró* [sacred] or *yeró* [strong, firm] and the *misó* [half]. An item common to them all is the wide-sleeved, full-length chemise, which is worn next to the skin[4] and is divided into the *emboústo* (close-fitting bodice) and *kormí* (literally, 'torso' or 'body', but in this case the skirt, gathered below the bust); typologically, therefore, it belongs to the category of chemises influenced by the Renaissance (Papantoniou 1978: 63) (fig. 6). Older chemises are made of linen and are therefore called *linarénia*, and the newer ones *vamvatsóla* (of cotton).

The chemises are decorated on their wide sleeves with embroideries reaching from the shoulder to the cuff. They fall into three groups, named after the type of embroidery used:

a) *skolopendráta*, which have strips of embroidery resembling centipedes [*Scolopendra* is a genus of centipedes] alternating with broader bands called *vétses*;

b) *kaliaráta*, which have *kaliáres* [little cockroaches] between narrow wavy bands;

c) *me tous díxous* [a corruption of *diskos*, 'discs' or 'trays'] – the *díxi* are described as 'circular motifs [...] a stylised and condensed representation of a flowerpot' (Zora 1969).

On the subject of the embroideries, Montesanto noted: 'The sleeves of the *skolopendráta* and the *kaliaráta* [...] are adorned on the inside with the characteristic motif of the third group, i.e. large *díxi*.' The *skolopendráta* do not have a 'right' and a 'wrong' side, a point taken up by Montesanto: 'This system is called *monoprósopo* (one-faced, or one-sided), and the designs are embroidered directly on to the cloth from the drawings, [...] without the lines being first traced onto the material. [...] The *kaliaráta*, on the other hand, [...] are embroidered using a system called *panoschediá*, meaning that they have a "right" and a "wrong" side. The chemise *me tous díxous* [...] may be embroidered in either way.' (Montesanto 1930?: 27-28; cf. Wace & Laurence 1914; Tarsouli 1996; Zairi 2001: 62). The sleeves of the chemise are so wide that they get in the way of any kind of work and even make it difficult to get dressed. For that reason, they always have a *vouklí* (cord) sewn into them on the inside, which allows the sleeve to be folded and kept in place behind the back for practical reasons (Montesanto 1930?:

Fig. 4. Mrs Helen Wace wearing a *chrysomándilo* costume that matches the detailed description given in the catalogue of the 1914 London exhibition. However, the *bólia* (long scarf) is incorrectly placed, probably from ignorance, so that it covers the *chrysomándilo* frontlet.
Benaki Museum Photographic Archive, Athens

28; Tarsouli 1996: 37). The hem of the chemise is embroidered with decorative motifs – sailing ships, trees, mounted camels, partridges, etc. – worked in a crude cross-stitch (Wace & Laurence 1914: XX; Montesanto 1930?: 30 and illus. 24-25; Tarsouli 1996: 36; Zairi 2001: 56-62.) The stitches used in these embroideries are beyond the scope of this article.

The *chrysomándilo* costume takes its name from the frontlet of its headdress and is always worn with a *skolopendráto* chemise, over which is worn a sleeved dress (sometimes called the *veloúdo*, literally 'velvet') (fig. 3). For a description of this type of dress, we cannot do better than to quote from the earliest publication of it, in the catalogue of an exhibition of 1914 in London (Wace & Laurence 1914). It is item number 81, lent to the exhibition by Mrs Theodore Bent and A. J. B. Wace. The accurate description that follows, by Wace himself, corresponds exactly to the costume shown in a photograph in the Benaki Museum, Athens, dated 1930, with a note to the effect that the lady in the photograph is Mrs Helen Wace (fig. 4).

Southern Sporades (Astypalaea)

Complete Bridal Costume consisting of an embroidered frock with plastron, over-skirt and headdress of a cap, frontlet and two kerchiefs.

The frock, which is of 4 widths, is embroidered in stitches, which comprise Italian two-sided cross-stitch, double running, and outline-stitch with coloured silks on linen. Round the bottom of the skirt is a continuous frieze of five-legged peacocks, all looking to the right. This pattern also runs a short distance up the sides of the seams which are joined at the bottom, where they would show below the over-skirt, with narrow bands of needlework. Over the shoulders runs a narrow border of hut-like objects. The sleeves are oblong and heavily gathered in at the shoulders where the joints are marked by a narrow line of embroidery picked out by gold threads. The sleeves are covered all over with a pattern consisting of alternating lines of irregular zigzag and rows of leaves set in pairs on a central stem. At the bottom is a red band with a wavy pattern reserved in the colour of the linen. The seams are marked by a row of devices locally called 'Trays' in blue. There is no embroidery down the V, but the opening is covered by a separate garment. This is an oblong plastron embroidered in silk and wool on linen with a pattern of pairs of leaves. At the top is a border of beads and gold thread, and the whole surface with sequins of coloured tin.

The over-skirt is of green satin with short sleeves trimmed with red satin and gold thread. Down the centre of the back of the body are three vertical rows of similar trimming. Under each arm behind is a bunch of silver charms to avert the evil eye. The bottom of the over-skirt is edged inside with a band of thick flannel in order to produce pleats which are much admired.

The headdress consists of a small peaked cap of red satin on which there is applied in front a double eagle flanked by a pair of peacocks. These are worked in gold and silver threads and are decorated with glass jewels and beads. Round the bottom of the cap in front runs a broad frontlet worked in gold thread with artificial rosettes attached just above the ears. Twisted round the cap and hanging in a long loop down the front is a long kerchief of cotton dyed in saffron, the ends of which are embroidered in cross and tent stitch in silk and gold with a wavy floral pattern. Attached to the cap behind is a similar long kerchief hanging down the back, which has all round a border of trees worked in tent stitch. Attached to the ends are extra borders embroidered in cross-stitch in coloured silk on linen with a frieze of men. Round the waist is a metal belt, and round the neck and on the headdress are silver chains.

Wace described the costume in detail, seeing it with the experienced eye of an archaeologist and art historian. Only occasionally did he use the English equivalent of the Greek word (for example, he calls the *díxi* 'trays'); and he referred to the partridges in the embroideries as 'peacocks'.

Fig. 7. The *chrysomándilo* costume. Note the cap with the double-headed eagle, the *chrysomándilo* frontlet, the *emboliá asiméni*, the *panomoustouchiá*, the *kombovelónes* and the *garýfala*. Late 19th century. Lyceum Club of Greek Women, Athens

Here it should be added that the *chrysomándilo* dress is made up of three parts: the *ambediá* (or *ambétia*), the *embliá* (or *émblia, embleá*) and the hem. The *ambediá* is a bodice to which the sleeves are attached. The *embliá* is a pleated skirt ending in a flounce, with the embroidered hem of the chemise visible below it. Wace mentioned the cluster of decorative metal pendants sewn on to the back of the dress, the so-called *koudoúnia tis armatosiás* (literally, 'bells of the armour'), but without specifying the names of their different shapes, such as *kástana, foundoúkia, kambánes* or *velanídia* (chestnuts, hazelnuts, bells, acorns) (Passa-Kotsou 1996; Zairi 2001: 61). Nor did he single out the *tsoúla* (the emblematic triangular pendant), which is mentioned specifically in a dowry contract of 1872 (Tarsouli 1996: 31) (figs 5-6).

It is also worth giving the names of the various parts of the headdress: *skoúfia* (cap), *chrysomándilo* (frontlet), *emboliá asimeni*[5] ('long silver headscarf') and *panomoustouchiá* (outer kerchief); this last is secured with *kombovelónes* (long silver pins with a spherical head) and *garýfala* (artificial flowers) (fig. 7). The *skoúfia*, incidentally, makes it necessary for the hair to be parted in the middle, with locks hanging down on either side of the forehead (Tarsouli 1996: 36).

Missing from Wace's description – and presumably from the costume shown in the 1914 exhibition – are the *chrysés vétses* (red stockings trimmed with gold braid) and the *chrysí fellí* (gold-embroidered mules) (figs 6, 8). Those are the first items to be put on, for obvious practical reasons (Tarsouli 1996: 35; PFF interview 1985). In figure 4, Mrs Wace is wearing pumps; moreover – probably from ignorance, and despite the fact that the headdress is correctly described in the text – she has the frontlet covered by the yellow kerchief.

The *skléta* is the 'second-best' festive costume; it is worn with a *kaliaráto* chemise (fig. 9). Here, the main garment is the *koutsomániko*, a silk or satin dress, with pleats or gathers and a broad flounce and with a cotton lining; it is sleeveless and backless and is held up by a pair of broad shoulder straps called the *ambediá*. Over the *koutsomániko* is worn the *goúna*,

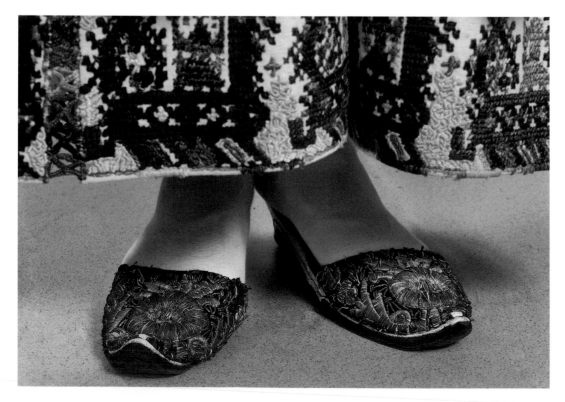

Fig. 8. The hem of a *skolopendráto* chemise with embroidered 'mounted camels'. Late 19th century. Lyceum Club of Greek Women, Athens

Fig. 9. Hand-coloured photograph of a *skléta* costume, by Émile Lester. Early 1920s.
Lyceum Club of Greek Women Photographic Archive, Athens

a short, sleeveless jacket of velvet or satin, fastened over the chest with *voukliá* (silken cords) (Montesanto 1930?: 31).

In the *skléta*, the headdress has no *chrysomándilo* frontlet, and the cap is fastened onto a rope circlet, the *boumbári* (Tarsouli 1996: 37). Next come two kerchiefs: the first, of yellow silk, holds the *boumbári*, cap and hair in place, while the second, also yellow,[6] is wound round the head like a turban and tied on the right temple in two bows, the *foúndes*. Ornamental metal pendants worn with the *skléta* include the *psaráki* (fish), *thikári* (scabbard), *klidákia* (keys) and *velonothíka* (needle case), which hang from the girdle (Montesanto 1930?: 32; Papamanoli 1986: 13).

Fig. 10. Three women in everyday dress, with three children. The costume of the woman in the middle is probably the *ieró*.
Photo: Wace, 1909.
Benaki Museum Photographic Archive, Athens

The only person to give fairly full particulars of the *ieró* or *yeró*, the third type of costume, is Montesanto (Montesanto 1930?: 32, 40-41): a purple *kaliaráto* chemise worn with a red *koutsomániko* dress, a red *goúna* and *nétes emboliés* (long, plain, undecorated kerchiefs) over the cap. On weekdays the *koutsomániko* was worn inside-out to avoid wear and tear on the 'right' side, 'and so it presents a different appearance and the inside-out version includes a green apron and a white hem (the lining material), while the inside remains red' (Montesanto 1930?: 32) (fig. 10). Irini (Rinaki) Palatianou, born in 1914, gave a very vivid description of the red *koutsomániko* with its white hem that her mother used to wear on weekdays, noting that even when in mourning – when the yellow kerchiefs were replaced with black ones – the women still wore the red dress. The long, wide sleeves, narrow at the wrist, served as pockets on weekdays (PFF interview 1985).

Lastly, we come to the *misó*, which Montesanto described as 'the least highly rated costume, worn by old women and married women' (Montesanto 1930?: 32). It comprises a chemise with *díxi*, a red woollen *embliá* with a green hem, a green apron sewn on to the skirt, a *goúna* of green velvet or red satin and a stole embroidered with woollen thread (fig. 1). It should be noted that most of the everyday dresses were made of felt (Passa-Kotsou 1996).

Of these four types of Astypalaian costume, the first two are the ones mentioned most often in the literature on the subject (Wace & Laurence 1914; Montesanto 1930?; Tarsouli 1996; Hatzimichali 1954; Papantoniou 1996; Minotou-Lada & Gangadi 2005). The *chrysomándilo* is generally described as a 'bridal dress' and the *skléta* as 'festive'. Montesanto, on the other hand, connected the *chrysomándilo* with the island's ruling class (of Venetian descent). Tarsouli, too, recalled an air of 'old nobility' about Astypalaia, but only in general terms: she made no attempt to draw distinctions between the different social classes as far as costume is concerned.

Nonetheless, when traditional costumes are under discussion, one is always aware of class distinctions. In the words of Rinaki Palatianou (PFF interview 1985): 'When we were invited to a wedding and the bride had [from] 12 [to] 6 girls [i.e. bridesmaids], we came out of the castle and walked down. Our heels clacked, the bells on our backs tinkled, [...] that's called the *tsoúla*, [...] as you walk it jingles.' She can only have been talking about the *chrysomándilo*, because that is the only costume that has bells and the *tsoúla*.[7] In fact, Rinaki's mother, Maria (Maroulaki) Palatianou, née Oikonomidi (1892-1972), came from 'a very good family, one of the best on Astypalaia, [...] from inside the castle [...]. She said there was a kingdom here, a palace in the village. There were 12 families, and my mother came from one [of] the 12.' Rinaki's mother wore the costume of Astypalaia for about 40 years, 'until the fourth child', that is, until the 1930s. 'She had worn out lots of clothes!' her daughter added. Actually, Rinaki, too, often wore the *chrysomándilo*, at various festivals and when standing as *koumbara* (a bride's principal attendant), although she herself was unmarried. This means that the *chrysomándilo* is not necessarily a bridal costume: it is also a mark of a woman's social status. These two forms of costume, *chrysomándilo* and *skléta*, coexisted in the established order of precedence of festive wear. 'The bride wears the *chrysomándilo*. When she changes, [...] she puts on her second wedding dress, the *skléta* [...] the same day [...]. [The *chrysomándilo*] is very heavy, the other is light,' Rinaki confirmed (PFF interview 1985).

The *chrysomándilo* acquired by the Peloponnesian Folklore Foundation from Rinaki Palatianou in 1985 goes back four generations, all the way to her great-grandmother, who must have been born around 1850. Hence the *chrysomándilo* embroidered by her great-grandmother can be dated to the 1870s or 1880s. This is consistent with the report that,

'The last [such] costume [...] was made in the castle (1890) with materials bought from a merchant named Askadeff, who travelled round the islands by ship'.[8] Another interesting point is that Rinaki Palatianou lent a *chrysomándilo* to her aunt, Kali Hadjiantoniou, for her to wear when she went with other ladies from the Dodecanese to the wedding of Crown Prince Umberto of Italy (the future Umberto II) in 1930 (PFF interview 1985; Papantoniou 1996: 92).

All in all, in the literature on the subject, the *chrysomándilo* and the *skléta* are described respectively as a 'bridal' and a 'festive' costume, following the generally accepted view that the differences between the costumes in the matter of costliness and ornamentation are associated with their ranking on the social scale, whether in the life of the community (festive occasion or everyday) or in the woman's own life (bride, newlywed, woman 'of a certain age', old woman or widow). Very little is written about everyday clothes. In conclusion, it is the interviews with islanders that suggest that the different types of Astypalaian costume reflect the *old* social stratification.

NOTES

1. So, too, did Angeliki Hatzimichali in her seminal work on Greek costumes, which was published in 1948, the same year in which Athina Tarsouli's book first appeared.

2. According to the dedicatory inscription on the castle wall, Giovanni IV Querini, Count of Astynea (not Astypalaia), brought the first colonists to the island on 30 March 1413 (see, for example, Tarsouli 1996: 23). The history of the Venetian occupation of Astypalaia is recounted in Miller, William, *The Latins in the Levant: A History of Frankish Greece (1204-1566)*, New York, E. P. Dutton & Co., 1908, a standard source for all writers since then.

3. A. J. B. Wace (1879-1957) was, among various other posts, Director of the British School at Athens (1914-1923), Keeper of Textiles at the Victoria and Albert Museum (1924-1934), Professor of Classical Archaeology, Cambridge (1934-1944), and Professor of Classics and Archaeology, Farouk 1 University, Alexandria.

4. It is also called the *tsopoukámiso* (Tarsouli 1996: 35). Virginia (Vergousaki) Makryllou, born in 1922, explained: 'A fine silk garment is worn next to the skin to cover the arm. It is fastened at the wrist.' (Passa-Kotsou 1996; PFF interview 1985). See figs 1, 10 herein.

5. The *emboliá asiméni* is dyed with saffron, which is gathered 'from the feast of the Taxiarchs [8 November] to the feast of St Nicholas [6 December]. The [saffron] crocus does not grow all over the island, but only on the mountain on the road to Ai-Yannis. We start at night and we have a great party!' Oral testimony of Virginia (Vergousaki) Makryllou (Passa-Kotsou 1996).

6. According to Montesanto, one of the two kerchiefs is white (Montesanto 1930?: 31).

7. Cf. the marriage settlement of 1872 (Tarsouli 1996: 31), in which the bride's dowry includes a house in the castle and a *chrysomándilo* costume.

8. From the inscription on a photograph (no. 46339) in the Benaki Museum, Athens, showing a *chrysomándilo* costume.

I wish to extend my warm thanks to Evangelia Antzaka-Vei, Hara Deligianni, Giorgos Goutis, Themelina Haralambopoulou, Anastasia Kotsou, Georgia Panselina, Maria Papadopoulou, Maria Papamichalopoulou, Tania Veliskou and Maria Vlachopoulou, for their time, valuable advice and insightful comments.

The 'Amalia' Costume:
The Visual Symbol of the Transition from the Oriental Past to Western Modernity (19th Century)

Nadia Macha-Bizoumi

On 22 November 1836, in the great hall of the palace at Oldenburg, Germany, a marriage took place between Amalia, daughter of Grand Duke Paul Friedrich August of Oldenburg, and King Otto of Greece. In the spring of 1837 the royal couple landed at Piraeus and drove to Athens, the new capital of the fledgling Greek kingdom. Amalia arrived wearing a fashionable white silk dress and a huge picture hat, also white (Bouse 2007: 34); Otto, following the advice of his father, King Ludwig I of Bavaria, chose to wear the foustanella (the Greek short pleated kilt).

During those early years after the War of Independence, Greece was in a state of social flux, for the population included people of Greek descent from many different countries (Skopetea 1988: 43). Establishing a national identity for the newly independent state now stood as a matter of vital importance. The new country's sovereignty – and hence its viability – could be assured by developing a collective ideology, thanks to which the members of this heterogeneous mosaic of humanity would acknowledge one another as belonging to the same nation and sharing the same culture, 'where culture in turn means a system of ideas and signs and associations and ways of behaving and communicating' (Gellner 1992: 23).

Fig 1. Chromolithograph depicting the arrival of King Otto and Queen Amalia in Athens.
Peloponnesian Folklore Foundation, Nafplio

Queen Amalia in her garden, *c.* 1855. Lithograph by Franz Hanfstaengl, based on the oil painting by Ernst Rietschel.
National Historical Museum, Athens

Gem. v. E. Rietschel.   Druck und Verlag v. P. Hartwig in München   Lith. v. H. Neubschmid

AMALIE KOENIGIN VON GRIECHENLAND.   ΑΜΑΛΙΑ ΒΑΣΙΛΙΣΣΑ ΤΗΣ ΕΛΛΑΔΟΣ.

The royal couple, recognising the need to create a unifying symbol, established a new sartorial idiom based on court dress, which gave visual expression to the ideological trends of the 19th century. Essentially, this involved the creation of two ensembles (fig. 1) which Otto and Amalia chose deliberately to suit that particular moment in history, when Europe was showing widespread interest in the popular cultures of the newly independent states (Macha-Bizoumi 2012: 66-67).

In establishing the Greek national identity and developing its visual image, Otto played his part by opting to appear in public wearing the foustanella, which was adopted before long as a form of urban dress (Droulia 1999: 136). The foustanella functioned as an expressive idiom, 'which transcended national and linguistic divisions and eventually came to be accepted as a garment definitive of Greek nationality and no other' (Bada 1995: 139, Verinis 2005: 139-175, Skafidas 2009: 145-163). Queen Amalia, for her part, devised a form of dress (Macha-Bizoumi 2012: 65-68) known as the 'Amalia' costume, inspired both by contemporary European fashion and by Greek traditional costume. The 'Amalia' costume served as 'an elaborate language of symbolic practice and communication' (Hobsbawm 2010: 14), a costume charged with ideological connotations and identified with the national costume of Greek women. Its composition was based on an extremely well-judged marriage of Eastern and Western sartorial elements. This single act, seen in direct association with the overall 'modernistic' policy of building a new sovereign state along Bavarian lines – a policy that 'attempted to import the institutions of a free European state into the Kingdom of Greece' (Kitromilides 2000: 35) – helped the newly formed Greek kingdom make the transition from its Oriental past to Western modernity.

What was the fashion prevailing in ladies' dress in Athens before Queen Amalia arrived? A clear picture of that is given by the lithograph entitled *Mariage grec à Athènes* (Greek wedding in Athens) by Louis Dupré (1825) (fig. 2 [detail]; see also p. 208). That print, as Papantoniou (2000: 270) was the first to point out, depicts a number of people all dressed in different styles. The central figure is an Athenian bride dressed in the Oriental urban fashion, wearing an *anderí*, a long-sleeved, ankle-length coat dress, scalloped all round and with a vertical opening at the front; this is worn over a chemise and long, wide breeches (*vráka*) and is covered by a short, pale blue coat trimmed with white fur. Round her hips is a broad, striped girdle. On her right (the viewer's left) stands a woman dressed in *arvanítika*, the type of costume worn by country women in most of Attica, with the characteristic *foúndi*, a sleeveless ankle-length chemise, richly decorated on the hem. This woman wears a tight bodice (*dzákos*) with lavishly embroidered sleeves and a white coat with red trimmings. On the bride's left (the viewer's right) are two women, each wearing a *feredzés* (a sort of over garment): one of them, mostly hidden, is obviously a Muslim, as she is wearing a white headscarf that covers the lower part of her face; the other, a Christian, wears a very long stole.

Fig. 2. Louis Dupré, *Mariage grec à Athènes* (Greek wedding in Athens), 1825 (detail; see illus., p. 208). Alpha Bank Photographic Archive, Athens

Fig 3. Photo of the court of Queen Amalia in 1847 by Philibert Perraud. National Historical Museum Photographic Archive, Athens

Fig. 4. The 'Amalia' dress. Late 19th – early 20th century. Museum of the History of Greek Costume, Lyceum Club of Greek Women, Athens

On the royal couple's arrival in Athens, the repertoire of costumes was broadened through the introduction of the foreign styles of people of various origins (Phanariots [Constantinopolitan Greeks, many of whom rose to high office and amassed great wealth under the Ottomans], members of the king's personal entourage, Western travellers, Jewish merchants and others) who had flocked to the new capital. Amongst the homespun *arvanítika* costumes could now be seen gossamer gowns made by Parisian couturiers, mostly worn by Phanariot ladies, who set the trend in the new social circles of Athens (Gatopoulos 1942). In fact, articles devoted to the latest Paris fashions started to appear in magazines of this period (Karpozilou 1991: 37).

To this varied scene Amalia added a touch of her own: she asked those of her ladies-in-waiting who were related to famous fighters of the Greek Revolution to wear the traditional costumes of their respective places of origin (fig. 3). Gennaios Kolokotronis' wife, Fotini, the daughter of Fotos Tzavellas, decided on an outfit that was a cross between the Souliot and Peloponnesian costumes; Kyriakoula Kriezi (see p. 151), the daughter of Georgios Voulgaris, bey of Hydra, and wife of Admiral Antonios Kriezis, opted for the local costume of Hydra, as did Kondylo Miaouli, daughter of Georgios Koundouriotis and wife of Athanasios Miaoulis, who was one of King Otto's aides-de-camp and Prime Minister of Greece; Maria Monarchidou, the daughter of Admiral Nikolis Apostolis of Psara, wore the costume of that island. This was the way in which Queen Amalia chose to honour the potent symbols of the Greek Revolution of 1821.

Another of Amalia's initiatives was to devise a Romantic, 'folkloric' costume consisting of three main garments – chemise, dress (fig. 4) and short jacket (fig. 5) – which she ordered her ladies-in-waiting to wear. The whole ensemble relied on a judicious blend of Western fashion ideas with elements taken from recent Greek tradition. This insistence on uniformity of dress for the ladies-in-waiting, in the form of the 'Amalia' costume (fig.

6), may be seen as a symbolic attempt to put in place a standard ensemble directly associated with Greek nationality.

A study of the main garments of the 'Amalia' costume leads to the following observations:

a) For the construction of the dress, the queen sought out ideas from clothing styles with which she was familiar. For that very reason, the skirt, which formed the lower part of the dress that she designed herself, was clearly influenced by a Romantic yet simple fashion, the Biedermeier style, which was extremely popular in 19th-century Germany and Austria. The fashionable clothes she herself wore conformed to that style. However, the close-fitting bodice of the 'Amalia' dress takes its shape and cut from the *kavádi* worn by society ladies in the Greek capital, which was modelled on Oriental fashions. The *kavádi* of the Athenian costume was a short-waisted dress with a close-fitting bodice, long, wide sleeves and a vertical opening at the front, fastened below the bust with silver or gilt filigree buttons. The wide sleeves were open at the sides to show the embroidery on the sleeves of the chemise (fig. 7 [detail]; see also p. 206). Out of this marriage of Oriental and Western elements was born the long gown or *kavádi* of the 'Amalia' costume, which was made of silks often decorated with woven-in floral motifs and/or embroidered with gold thread.

b) Another borrowing from the traditional Athenian costume was the *zipoúni* or *kondogoúni*, which in the early 1820s took the form of a short, very low-necked jacket

Fig. 5. *Kondogoúni* of the 'Amalia' costume.
Museum of the History of Greek Costume, Lyceum Club of Greek Women, Athens

hugging the chest tightly. I should mention here that at that time the *zipoúni* or *kondogoúni* was worn throughout mainland Greece and the islands (fig. 8), with variations from place to place, so there was every reason for this widely distributed garment to be taken as the basis for the *zipoúni* of the 'Amalia' (fig. 5). The *zipoúni* or *kondogoúni* of the 'Amalia' was a jacket with long, tight sleeves, made of silken velvet in black, red or dark blue, sewn and embroidered by specialist tailors called *terzídes*, with silken cords (sometimes of gold or silver thread) attached. It was often adorned with fur all round.

c) Western-style ornaments such as cameo brooches, diamond brooches, cameo medallions, diamond bracelets and strings of pearls put the finishing touches to the ensemble.

Fig. 6. The 'Amalia' costume.
Early 20th century.
Peloponnesian Folklore Foundation,
Nafplio

Fig. 7. Gerasimos Pitzamanos,
Athenian Lady with her Young Daughter,
1818 (detail; see illus., p. 206).
Note the *kavádi*.
National Historical Museum, Athens

Fig. 8. A *zipoúni* of the island type,
from Hydra.
Late 19th – early 20th century.
Museum of the History of Greek
Costume, Lyceum Club of Greek
Women, Athens

Fig. 9. Embroidery on silk by Maria Briakou with portraits of King Otto and Queen Amalia,
c. 1837, 35.5 x 38.5 cm.
Museum of the City of Athens – Vouros-Eutaxias Foundation

d) The head was covered with a cap (a low fez) like the ones worn with the Athenian costume, with gold embroidery and a silk tassel (the *papazi*) of plaited gold threads (fig. 6), often decorated with pearls or spangles. Papantoniou (2000: 391) notes that the women covered the cap with a black lace mantilla when they went to church.

It should come as no surprise to learn that Queen Amalia borrowed certain elements from the clothes worn by Athenian society ladies. In fact, at least in the early years of Otto's reign, she herself would doubtless have worn the traditional Athenian costume. This was modelled on Oriental forms of dress: the outfit consisted of *salivária* (long, baggy breeches), a chemise, a floor-length dress with a vertical opening (the *kavádi*) and often another, shorter dress over the *kavádi*. Depending on the season and the circumstances of use, a short or long coat dress – long-sleeved, short-sleeved or sleeveless (*anderí*, *tsipoúni* or *dzoumbés*) – might be worn on top of the whole ensemble. The *dzoumbés*, which was made of expensive material and fur-lined, was worn only by upper-class ladies. The Museum of the City of Athens has in its collection a piece of embroidery made around 1837, depicting the royal couple in half length on their wedding day, with the king wearing a foustanella and the queen dressed in the Athenian costume with *kavádi* and *dzoumbés* (fig. 9).

It was only on special occasions that Amalia appeared in public wearing the costume she devised herself, an ensemble closely associated with her Greek royal status. The current state of research indicates that she, unlike Otto, preferred to wear fashionable Parisian clothes at court, rather than the ensemble she herself had created (Macha-Bizoumi 2012: 72-73). It should be noted that the project of establishing a form of dress clearly connected with Greek nationality was backed up by a series of specially commissioned portraits showing the queen in Greek national costume (von Hase-Schmundt 2007: 257-268, Kasimati 2000: 520).

Queen Amalia created a form of dress that served as an elaborate 'language' of symbolic practice and communication (Lurie 1983, Rubinstein 1995) to make known the identity of the Modern Greek state. The design of this Romantic national costume renders in visual terms the 19th-century ideological trends that influenced its conception, for it is charged with symbolic and ideological connotations. The 'Amalia' was a landmark in the history of Greek fashion: it endured for a considerable length of time and inspired the creation of a number of 'Amalianised' styles (Papantoniou 2000: 391) (fig. 10), which gained ascendancy over earlier forms of dress not only in Greece, but in the Balkans generally and Serbia in particular (Antonijević 1983: 343-353, Vitković-Žikić 2009: 118-123). At first it was worn only in the cities and towns, but after a time it was taken up in rural areas as well.

However, the strong progress of this costume created by Queen Amalia should certainly not be seen as the march of 'fashion', as that term is used in the world of *haute couture*, for it was a form of dress devised and made as a symbol of the Modern Greek state, tantamount to a uniform, and that is the very reason why it was so widely adopted. However, it did play an intermediary role in the diffusion and adoption of Western styles, whereby – initially through the agency of Queen Amalia and later, more forcefully, of Queen Olga – Western fashions gradually prevailed in Greece.

Fig. 10. Photo of Ourania Negri wearing an 'Amalianised' costume of Samos, 1910.
Private collection

The Costume of the Ladies-in-Waiting to Queen Olga:
Court Elegance Using Local Materials

Xenia Politou

Olga, a Grand Duchess of Russia and member of the Romanov dynasty, was born on 3 September 1851 in the Pavlovsk Palace near St Petersburg. A daughter of Grand Duke Konstantine Nikolayevich and Grand Duchess Alexandra Iosifovna (born Princess Alexandra of Saxe-Altenburg), she was married in 1867, at the age of 16, to King George I of the Hellenes and thus became Queen of Greece. Olga was on the throne for 46 years (1867-1913), until her husband's assassination in 1913. Thereafter, apart from a short period in 1920 when she was regent, she divided her time among Russia, Switzerland, Great Britain, France and Italy, where she died on 18 June 1926. She left behind her a great legacy of good works, having founded hospitals and charitable institutions and been patroness of numerous schools, mostly for young girls.

One of her priorities on becoming Queen of the Hellenes was to learn Greek, which demonstrates her willingness to adapt to her new role. The same attitude could account for her initiative in creating an official costume for her ladies-in-waiting, inspired by Greek local costumes (fig. 1). In this, she would appear to have been following the example of her German predecessor, Amalia, the first Queen of Greece, who devised a form of court dress that combined contemporary European fashion trends with features of traditional Greek costumes.

The same philosophy was also to be found in the formal dress of the Russian court, with which Olga was undoubtedly familiar. The dress code for ladies at the Russian court, laid down by Nicholas I's Edict on Court Dress of 1833, remained in effect, with some modifications, until 1917. It combined the Romantic style of that period with Russian tradition. The main garment of the ensemble was a gold-embroidered velvet coat dress with long, wide sleeves that could be thrown back over the shoulders – a characteristic feature of the old Russian costume – and a skirt with a long train. This garment seems to have been inspired by the *sarafan*, the long, straight coat dress of the traditional Russian costume (Nicholson 2013). With the narrowing of the waistline and the addition of the train, 'According to an apt remark of a contemporary, the costume reminded one of a "Frenchified" *sarafan*.' (Alyoshina *et al*. 1977: 25). The 'Frenchified' *sarafan* was worn over an embroidered white silk dress, part of which was visible, as the *sarafan* was open

Fig. 1. Queen Olga
with her ladies-in-waiting, *c*. 1885.
National Historical Museum
Photographic Archive, Athens

down to the waist at the front. The gown was supplemented by a *kokoshnik*, the typical headdress of the Russian costume, which in the court version was more like a diadem, and a white veil (fig. 2).

The idea of creating a form of court dress that combined the local tradition and official palace fashion was therefore not unknown to Queen Olga. Having adopted the basic structure of Russian court dress, she turned to Greek traditional costume to select the features that would give the new outfit the Greek character she sought. Moreover, her interest in Greek costumes was not limited to drawing inspiration from them for the design of the new court dress: it manifested itself in a variety of other ways as well. Of these, it is worth mentioning her initiative in making a collection of dolls dressed in exact replicas of Greek costumes, her ultimate intention being to found a museum of costumes in miniature.[1]

In devising the dress to be worn by the ladies-in-waiting at her court, Olga looked to the costume tradition of the villages of northern and eastern Attica, from Lavrion to the foothills of Mount Parnitha, the best-known region being the Mesogeia (the inland area of the Attic peninsula). The bridal or festive costume of Attica was extremely popular in the high society of the capital at the time, as evidenced by numerous studio photos of Athenian ladies: photographers usually had in their studio a festive costume from somewhere in Attica to satisfy the Athenian ladies' desire to be photographed as village girls against the background of an idyllic or archaic scene set up for the purpose (Papantoniou 1998: n.p.) (fig. 3).

In point of fact, when we talk about the elements Queen Olga borrowed for her court dress from the festive costume of Attica, we should limit ourselves to two items: the woollen waistcoat (the *gríza*, to give it its local name) and the headdress, which includes an ornamental frontlet like a diadem called the *xelítsi* or *koronátsi* and an all-silk *bólia* (a long, narrow scarf that goes over the head).

Turning to the way these elements were incorporated into a court dress code, we see that the Greek court dress follows the structure of the Russian, with the difference that the main garments of the Russian costume were replaced by the corresponding Greek-inspired garments. First of all, the place of the Russian long velvet coat dress was taken by a woollen waistcoat modelled on the *gríza* of the Mesogeia region.

Fig. 3. Woman wearing the costume of Attica in an Athenian photographer's studio, *c.* 1875. Photo: Petros Moraitis. Modern Greek Historical Collection of Konstantinos Tripos – Benaki Museum Photographic Archive, Athens

Fig. 2. Vladimir Makovsky, *Portrait of Maria Feodorovna, Empress of Russia, Wife of Tsar Alexander III*, 1885. State Russian Museum, St Petersburg

This garment was made of white felt, like the *gríza* (fig. 4), and is of about the same length: that is to say, it covers the hips and follows the same lines in its decoration, having broad bands of a different material all round the edges and gold couching embroidery (fig. 5). It even has – though with variations – the same decorative motif of appliqué gold-embroidered rosettes at the end of ornamental colonnettes which extend downwards from the armhole on the back of the *gríza*. Mainly, however, the court waistcoat differs from the *gríza* because, to conform to the style of court dress and current fashion, it was made narrower at the waist, often with the help of a small buckle to hold it together at the front. It also differs with regard to the sewn-on decorative borders: whereas in the *gríza* of the Mesogeia they may be made of either red felt or deep red or mauve velvet, in the waistcoat of the new court dress the borders are always of velvet. We learn from the memoirs of Christina Kosti, one of Olga's ladies-in-waiting, that the choice of colour for this velvet was subject to certain rules: it was red for members of the royal family and

Fig. 5. The *gríza*, the long, sleeveless waistcoat of the bridal costume of the Mesogeia region. Photo: Leonidas Kourgiantakis. Benaki Museum, Athens

Fig. 4. The waistcoat of the costume of Queen Olga's ladies-in-waiting. Peloponnesian Folklore Foundation, Nafplio

Fig. 6. The costume of Queen Olga's ladies-in-waiting. Peloponnesian Folklore Foundation, Nafplio

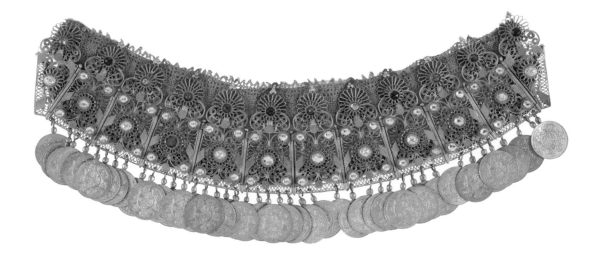

light blue for the ladies-in-waiting, while Athenian society ladies could choose any colour they liked other than those two (Kosti 1948-1949: 15-16).[2] Here again, Olga adopted a practice from the etiquette of the Russian court, where the colour of the velvet coat dress likewise indicated the wearer's position in the palace hierarchy and was not a matter of free choice (Alyoshina *et al*. 1977: 25).

As regards the designs of the gold embroideries and their arrangement on the waistcoat, it is safe to say that most are in the sinuous, curvilinear style commonly found in the couching work on the overdresses of Greek costumes (fig. 4). Such embroideries were usually worked with twisted gold thread or a silk (or, more rarely, woollen) twist, which was laid on the surface of the backing material without passing through it and held in place by small stitches of fine thread. The twisted thread followed the design drawn on the cloth, in a single continuous line. This technique also determined the style of the design, which was always curvilinear. Such gold embroidery was done professionally, and during the Turkish period the *terzídes*[3] organised themselves into guilds. They travelled all over Greece, taking with them not only the tools of their trade but also a common aesthetic approach to decoration (Zora 1994: 23). When Greece became independent and Westernised tailors introduced European fashions, the *terzídes* were renamed *ellinoráptes* (Greek tailors) and continued to work in the old way, though from the late 19th century they started using the recently invented sewing machine (Papantoniou 2006: n.p.). The technique of couched embroidery was still alive in Queen Olga's reign. The gold-embroidered waistcoats of the ladies-in-waiting would almost certainly have come from the hands of these experienced craftsmen; the designs would have been adapted to the personal taste of the lady concerned, even if that meant introducing new motifs such as the palmette[4] and, more frequently, the meander or 'Greek fret' (fig. 5); neither of these subjects was included in the *terzídes*' usual repertoire, but they reflect the aesthetic trend predominating in the Greek urban middle class at that time, which was Neoclassicism. The gold-embroidered waistcoat was too short to take the place of the velvet coat dress of the Russian court dress. To complete the ensemble, the waistcoat was combined with a skirt with a train, open at the front, which was made of the same materials and decorated in the same style (fig. 6).

Moving on to the next feature of the costume of Attica whose influence can be seen in the court dress of Olga's ladies-in-waiting, we shall see that the headdress of the

Fig. 9. The *bólia* (long scarf) of the bridal costume of Attica.
Photo: Leonidas Kourgiantakis.
Benaki Museum, Athens

Mesogeia costume was the source of inspiration for a diadem and kerchief that took the place of the Russian *kokoshnik* and the veil that goes with it. The decorated frontlet of the costume of Attica is not exactly a diadem, although it looks like one: it consists of a row of jointed lengths of filigree work with inlaid faux gemstones (fig. 7). It is attached to the inner kerchief by two hooks at the temples, and along the bottom it has a row of imitation coins adorning the forehead. This last is the feature that is found in the corresponding part of the court dress, which is a gilt diadem made of cast metal with a row of similar coins along the bottom. It is worn on the top of the head, often with an inner kerchief (fig. 8).

The accessory of Olga's court dress that it most reminiscent of the Mesogeia costume is the *bólia*, which is almost an exact replica (fig. 10). It is the same shape, is made of the same silk muslin in the natural colour of silk, like the Mesogeia *bólia*, and is likewise decorated at both ends with gold-thread bobbin lace and long fringes, also of gold thread. The only difference is the absence of the gold or silk embroideries that adorn the Mesogeia *bólia* (fig. 9).

Regarding the last component of the costume, the underdress, we can say that both the Russian and the Greek court dress have a garment or set of garments, respectively, made of white silk, but without anything else in common. It is also true to say that the set of undergarments in the Greek court dress, worn under the woollen waistcoat, is quite different from the undergarment worn under the *gríza* of the Mesogeia costume, which is a sleeveless cotton chemise lavishly adorned with multicoloured and gold embroidery. In contrast to most Greek local costumes, where the basic garment is a long chemise, the undergarments in the court dress of Olga's ladies-in-waiting are a skirt (usually with a train) and a waist-length chemise with long, wide sleeves. Yet even so, in its own way, this ensemble reflects the influence of Greek costume-making, not in its form or structure, but in the materials and techniques used in its make-up and decoration. This

Fig. 10. The kerchief of Queen Olga's court dress.
Peloponnesian Folklore Foundation, Nafplio

set of undergarments is made of the same natural-silk-coloured silk muslin as the *bólia*, an almost transparent material thanks to its fine-spun silk thread and its loose weave. Its only decorative feature is the addition of woven-in ribs, either horizontal or vertical (that is, in line with the weft or the warp), of different materials: gold thread, boiled-silk thread, coarser silk thread or even cotton thread.

It should be mentioned here that weaving in Greece never attained the same technical standards as in the rest of Europe or in parts of the Ottoman Empire (Constantinople and Bursa). It remained at the level of a home handicraft and was limited to the use of two or four shafts for the production of tabby, taffeta or twill. Weaving silk cloth was one of the most advanced forms of this production, for the woven-in ribbing created a further difficulty for the weaver.[5] This type of striped material was used mainly for women's chemises in places where silk was produced or where this luxury item was obtainable. Silk was also the only material used for those substitutes for the woman's chemise found in many urban women's costumes, including the 'Amalia' costume, namely a chemisette and a pair of sleeves worn under the long-sleeved, long silk dresses. Lastly, this type of striped silk fabric was sometimes used for household linens, mostly sheets and pillowcases, and, of course, for the kerchiefs characteristic of the costumes of Attica and some places nearby: certain villages of Euboea and Boeotia, the Megara area, Salamis and elsewhere.

In the surviving examples[6] of Olga's court dress, we find an interesting variety of striped materials: with horizontal or vertical stripes, alternating broad and narrow stripes, stripes of gold thread or thicker silk thread. These materials attest to the existence of a flourishing silk industry and are immediately recognisable to anyone who knows about Greek traditional costumes. This feeling of familiarity is strengthened by the decoration of these undergarments, because gold-thread bobbin lace, as used at the ends of the *bólia*, reappears as a decorative border on the cuffs, hem, collar and front neck opening and also runs in a seam-like line joining the two pieces of material forming the wide sleeves. This is a decorative approach widely used in the silk chemises of the Northern Sporades, in particular. Finally, in some rare examples of silk court garments the decoration is supplemented by a small or large zone of gold couching embroideries.

It is clear, then, that in addition to the structural features that Queen Olga's court dress borrowed from the costume of Attica, its chief debt to traditional Greek costumes lies in the materials and techniques used: striped silk cloth in the natural colour of silk, gold thread, couching embroidery and bobbin lace. The luxuriousness of the court dress owed nothing to imported materials or other imported products. At the very time when European silks were available in all Greek towns and imported patterns from the West were superseding the old embroidery designs and techniques (Papantoniou 1999: 50), Queen Olga turned to traditional ways to make the court dress for her ladies-in-waiting. In this way, she suggested that what is a luxury for a Greek country bride is good enough for the adornment of herself and her entourage, while simultaneously demonstrating her interest in Greek local costumes and the techniques used in making them.[7]

NOTES

1. With this in mind, in 1912-1913 Queen Olga ordered the dolls from London and then sent them to various parts of Greece to be dressed by the local people in exact copies of their traditional costumes. She then donated her collection to the newly founded Lyceum Club of Greek Women, Athens, where they remain to this day (Karolou 1934: 190-193; see also Papantoniou and Politou [eds] 2000: n.p.).

2. This contradicts the information from the National Historical Museum, Athens, that it has in its collections a costume from Queen Olga's court bordered with red velvet, which belonged to Angeliki Moraitini, née Mandzavinou. Perhaps future research will clear up this question.

3. The word *terzís* comes from the Turkish *terzi* (tailor), but in Greek it has the more specific meaning of professional tailors who specialised in gold couching embroidery.

4. The palmette (or anthemion) motif has been identified only on the costume of Sophia Alexandrou Soutzou, née Mavrokordatou, which is in the Benaki Museum, Athens.

5. Nikos Saltaris, in his study of the costume of Salamis, which includes the same type of *bólia* as that of Attica, describes the high level of skill required of the weavers of such kerchiefs if they were to achieve exactly the right tension in the warp, which was composed of threads of different kinds. Each kind of thread (silk or gold thread) required a different degree of tension according to its elasticity, otherwise the surface of the cloth would not be smooth (Saltaris 1986: 463-464).

6. The Benaki Museum, Athens, has nine full costumes and a number of accessories; the National Historical Museum, Athens, has three (Minotou-Lada & Gangadi 2005: 242-248); the Peloponnesian Folklore Foundation, Nafplio, has one full costume and some accessories (Papantoniou 2000: 274-279; Papantoniou & Kanellopoulos 1999: 86-89); the Museum of Greek Folk Art, Athens, has one; and the Kalamata branch of the Lyceum Club of Greek Women has one costume and a few accessories.

7. Queen Olga's secretary, Ioulia Karolou, wrote the following comments, which shed further light on this interest of hers: 'The Queen, whose mode of dress was very simple and practical, nearly always wore snow-white dresses. She ordered a cloth made of local materials, which was woven for her in the women's prisons, and to which she herself gave the name *karavópanon* (sailcloth), as well as another, finer cloth, also white, which was transparent and cooler. The latter was what she usually wore in summer, setting an example of extreme simplicity and supporting local production.' (Karolou 1934: 108-109).

Revisiting Greek Elegance:
Greek Local Costume as a Source of Inspiration for Contemporary Fashion and Costume Design

Sofia Pantouvaki

Greek costumes have often served as a source of inspiration for contemporary designers, not only in the field of fashion but also in theatrical costume design.

The earliest allusions to 'Greek' costume history in the morphology and aesthetics of Western garments appeared in the late 18th century, the period of the Classical Revival, and reappeared in the 19th century with the advent of Neoclassicism. These were features incorporating Romantic echoes of the tradition of classical antiquity. In the 19th century we find the first examples in Greece of garments combining Western fashion with forms of dress, ornamentation and/or accessories belonging to the Post-Byzantine Greek local traditions, at the instigation of Queen Amalia and Queen Olga, both of whom did their best to win the goodwill of their female Greek subjects using the language of dress: this aspect of the matter is discussed in other articles in this catalogue.

From around the turn of the 20th century, European fashion designers started harking back to the ancient Greek costumes of the Classical period, enchanted by the movement and chiaroscuro of the draperies. Some of the most characteristic examples drawing their inspiration from ancient Greek garments included dresses by Mariano Fortuny ('Delphos', 1907), Madeleine Vionnet (1920s and 1930s), Madame Grès (1930-1960), Jean Dessès (1940s and 1950s) and, much later – in an 'exchange of cultural assets' (Falida 2009: 4) – garments by the Japanese designer Issey Miyake (1980s) and Sophia Kokosalaki (since 1990). Within Greece, too, designers in the last few decades have used pleated drapery as a basic source of inspiration for their creations, not only in the field of couture but also in theatrical costume design (Pantouvaki 2009).

The expansion and promotion of research on Greek popular culture and the development of ethnography and folklore studies as academic disciplines coincided with the abandonment of local costumes for everyday town wear in nearly all parts of Greece by the mid-20th century. At the same time, townspeople became interested in adopting a new approach to local costumes with the aim of incorporating selected features of the traditional garments into the aesthetic of current fashion, as well as creating new fashions inspired by popular culture.

More specifically, from the mid-1950s a dialogue developed 'between the contemporary and the traditional', a dialogue that was presented as 'a suggested means of recreating the aesthetic codes of an idealised past' and was 'a symbolic way of voicing the urban middle-class nostalgia for the past' (Macha-Bizoumi 2010: 99). One of the first exponents of this trend was the Greek-Cypriot couturier Yiannis Evangelidis, who made an extensive study of Greek local costumes in the Benaki Museum in Athens and made good use of elements taken from the Neohellenic costume tradition, thus 'breathing new life into Athenian fashion' (PFF 2006, n.p.). The same spirit imbues the *haute couture* garments he created in the United States, where he worked later.

Fig. 1. Cape, handmade jacket, hand-woven skirt, necklace and kerchief, 2012. Created by Joanna Louca for the *Beyond Dress Codes* exhibition in Cyprus.
Photo: Filep Motwary

In the 1960s, the trend towards the creation of a Greek 'traditional fashion', which led to 'a very interesting presentation of Greek tradition and culture through the medium of clothes' (Tseklenis 2000: 14), became enormously popular. It was adopted by numerous Greek fashion designers and other creative artists, as in the case of Cleo's Boutique in the Hilton Hotel in Athens (Politou 2010: 7), sometimes in individual collections and sometimes in collective projects organised in collaboration with the National Organisation of Hellenic Handicrafts. The NOHH supported the efforts of Greek couturiers by setting up the necessary cooperative frameworks, which either laid emphasis on Greek decorative motifs drawn from the popular tradition or promoted the production of Greek textiles. This fashion was followed by the Lyceum Club of Greek Women (LCGW), which organised a series of fashion shows in the 1960s where they presented dresses made of woven materials, inspired by the local costumes of various parts of Greece (Macha-Bizoumi 2010). The presentation of the shows was imaginative: each mannequin modelling one of the new creations was accompanied by a member of the LCGW's dance group wearing the local costume from which it was derived.

The activities of the NOHH were continued by its successor, the Greek Organisation of Small and Medium-sized Companies and Handicrafts, known in English as HOMMEH, which organised projects of a similar kind throughout the 1980s and 1990s, the aim being always to focus attention on popular culture as an aesthetic point of reference for contemporary designers working in the field of fashion and fabrics. In 1985 HOMMEH published a coffee-table book presenting creations by Yannis Galatis from the 1960s and 1970s: 'I turned my attention to Greek woven fabrics, a hitherto neglected subject, and introduced them to foreign experts from all over the world,' says Galatis in his introduction to the book, with the purpose of 'persuading Greek women to love Greek fashions and forget about imported ones' (Galatis 1985: 5-6). Galatis' designs are typical of the trend for using popular art in the decoration of garments of disparate morphological origins, often by incorporating parts of the original costumes exactly as they are. Ioanna Papantoniou has written about 'the fashion designers' desperate determination to go back to the roots' at that time, a desire that 'was translated into what one might call a folkloristic approach' (Papantoniou 2010: 23). This method was viable even without specialised study of the cultural, social and economic parameters that gave rise to local costumes, but it was not marked by any particular creative dynamism.

A pioneer in the use of Greek elements in the design of materials and garments from a somewhat different point of view was Yannis Tseklenis. His work (1965-1990) includes thematic collections inspired by specific periods in the history of Greek art and popular handicrafts, covering the whole spectrum of Greek civilisation from the art of the Aegean Islands in early antiquity to Byzantine art and Greek wood-carving. His emphasis on Greek civilisation is evident not only in the themes of many of his collections, but also in the artistic direction of his new collections at fashion shows, photographs and films brilliantly illustrating Greek backgrounds inspired by the civilisation of Greece – even though the underlying theme of a given collection might not necessarily be Greek (Georgitsoyanni & Pantouvaki 2011: 157-158). Yet his inspiration did not concentrate specifically on the popular tradition: he sought above all to introduce a 'feeling of Greekness' in his designs, to create a fashion born of Greece. He himself describes his relationship with Greek tradition as 'strong, without ever turning into folklore' (Tseklenis 2002: 54).

Tseklenis' example was followed by other designers in the 1980s. However, they concentrated on more general and more abstract elements of Greece and Greek civilisation – such as whitewashed houses and the blue of the sea – rather than features of the popular cultural tradition, least of all on traditional local dress.

In the most recent generations of Greek fashion designers, the Greek element is reappearing, sometimes making its presence felt dynamically and sometimes remoulded and unobtrusively incorporated into the contemporary aesthetic. The way elements taken from the forms of traditional Greek local costumes and the connotations underlying them are approached, analysed, understood and interpreted is not always the same: it depends on the contemporary designer's personal relationship with those costumes. Every approach is based on the individual's own experience and conception of beauty and his or her knowledge of Greek local costumes and the cultural context in which they came into being. Sometimes, too, these costumes and their visual character – as natural objects with a specific form and cut, specific materials and decoration – have served as a direct visual reference point for new, imaginative dress designs, especially when foreign couturiers have turned to them in their quest for new sources of inspiration.

An interesting recent attempt to draw attention to these cases was the exhibition entitled *Beyond Dress Codes: From Traditional Costume to Contemporary Fashion*, organised by the Hellenic American Union and curated by the art and fashion historian Lydia Kamitsis. The idea for the exhibition arose from the drawings of local costumes and headdresses from various parts of Greece by Gisis Papageorgiou. Together with these, creations by contemporary Greek fashion designers were exhibited, including examples by Ioannis Guia, Yiorgos Eleftheriades, Sophia Kokosalaki, Thanos Kyriakides, Angelos Bratis, Dimitris Dassios, Orsalia Parthenis, Deux Hommes, Mastori*Motwary Studio and Mi-Ro, as well as the international couturiers Jean-Paul Gaultier and John Galliano. After opening in Athens (27 September – 27 October 2010, Hellenic American Union Gallery), the exhibition was taken on tour to Thessaloniki (4 December 2010 – 9 January 2011, Macedonian Museum of Contemporary Art) and Nicosia (27 September 2012 – 2 May 2013, Laiki Bank Cultural Centre). In Nicosia it was expanded, in collaboration with the Cyprus Fashion Designers Association, by the addition of designs by 17 Cypriot couturiers, who drew their inspiration from Cypriot traditional costumes and popular art (Vryonidou-Yiangou 2012: 20) (fig. 1). The titles of some of the reviews of the exhibition, especially those published after the first two showings in Athens and Thessaloniki, speak for themselves: 'My dear Evzone…' (Kusteni 2010), 'The Karagouna is back in fashion' (Falida 2010), 'When Hatzimichali met Gaultier' (Pissalidis 2010), 'When the foustanella is a source of inspiration!' (Gomouza 2010). [The Evzones are the Greek presidential guard, whose uniform includes a variation of the foustanella (short pleated kilt) originally worn by Greek fighters in the War of Independence; a Karagouna is a female native of the plains of Thessaly; Angeliki Hatzimichali was a famous Greek authority on popular culture.]

The designers taking part in the exhibition listed a wide range of features that had influenced them and also drew attention to the various alternative ways of interpreting folk costumes, which helped them to develop their different visual approaches. Thanos Kyriakides mentions that he was moved by 'the astonishing handiwork that has gone into [traditional local costumes] and the fact that this opulence used to be

a part of everyday life' (*Beyond Dress Codes* 2012: 28). The different interpretations of contemporary fashion designers, visually apparent in their designs, are also evident in the words they use to explain the thought processes underlying their approaches to traditional local costumes in their work: Sophia Kokosalaki refers to her 'abstract' approach (*ibid*. 35), the Mastori*Motwary Studio their 'experimental' approach (*ibid*. 37), Menelaos Meletiou the 'conjunction' of past and present (*ibid*. 46), the Atelier Loukia 'a mixture of details' (*ibid*. 41), the Parthenis fashion house the 'suggestive' role of their allusions (*ibid*. 33), the Deux Hommes 'a quieter, more discreet and, in the last analysis, more up-to-date feeling' (*ibid*. 39), and Ioannis Guia his searching for data 'by working with my eyes looking straight ahead and nowhere else' (*ibid*. 43). These keywords used by the designers themselves indicate the creative potential of the meeting between contemporary couturiers and the local costumes of Neohellenic culture.

There is also a place for subtle humour, as in the collection of the couturier Dimitris Dassios presented at the 6th Greek Fashion Week in October 2007, which he entitled 'Arta and Yannena' in self-mockery. He used this colloquial expression signifying an excessive array of heterogeneous objects, and hence the notion of exaggeration, because he deliberately overloaded his designs with miscellaneous accessories, including brooches and ornaments taken from Greek popular tradition (fig. 2).

An area of particular interest is the use of traditional Greek costume features by the international couturiers Jean-Paul Gaultier and John Galliano. Both of them, in recent collections, have used either the cut of the garments or parts of Greek popular decorative motifs or some of the accessories (jewellery, headdresses, etc.) that go with Greek local costumes.

Of the two, Jean-Paul Gaultier, well known for his love of Greece, is the more closely acquainted with Greek culture thanks to his frequent visits to the country, and more particularly Greek museums. In two of his recent collections, Gaultier was quite clearly inspired by 'Greek tradition'. In his Spring/Summer 2006 couture collection he showed, among other garments, some organza foustanella-dresses with very wide sleeves influenced by the shirt of the Evzones' uniform. According to *Vogue* (Morton 2006), the collection captured 'all the flavouring of the country', which Gaultier had absorbed on

Fig. 2. A creation of Dimitris Dassios from the 'Arta and Yannena' collection, 6th Greek Fashion Week, October 2007.
Photo: Patricia Munster.
Dimitris Dassios Archive

Fig. 3. Leather jacket incorporating decorated areas derived from the *fērmeli*. Jean-Paul Gaultier, Autumn-Winter 2010-2011 ready-to-wear collection.
Photo: Thanassis Krikis
Beyond Dress Codes: From Traditional Costume to Contemporary Fashion exhibition catalogue, co-organised by the Hellenic American Union, the Cyprus Fashion Designers Association and the Laiki Bank Cultural Centre, Nicosia 2012

his visits to Greece. In the same season he incorporated features taken from gold-embroidered cloaks into the ladies' waistcoats in his ready-to-wear collection. In his Autumn/Winter 2010-2011 ready-to-wear collection he showed a skirt based on the cut of the foustanella, as well as a jacket with decorated areas directly derived from the *férmeli* (the embroidered waistcoat worn with the foustanella) (fig. 3). In both cases he used a tasselled cap in the styling of the garments.

John Galliano, on the other hand, came across the Greek local costume tradition quite by chance in 2008, when he happened to visit the London branch of the Lyceum Club of Greek Women. Lydia Kamitsis takes up the story: 'His eye fell upon the Greek costumes. [...] He was so struck by them that he started looking for books and articles on the subject. His team got in touch with me, and I recommended the albums of photos of the Benaki Museum collection.' (Falida 2010). Galliano used explicit references to local costumes of northern Greece and the Aegean Islands in his Autumn/Winter 2009-2010 ready-to-wear collection. Affinities are to be seen both in the materials (e.g. felt) and in the ornaments and decorative designs (pompoms from peasants' handmade shoes, brooches and many other decorative motifs), and one even comes across almost perfect copies of the headdresses worn with various local costumes: from Gidas in Imathia, from Stefanoviki in Magnesia (figs 4a-4b) and from the island of Astypalaia (figs 5a-5b). The numerous imaginative ideas used in this collection

Figs 4a-4b and 5a-5b. Accessories and headgear from John Galliano's Autumn-Winter 2009-2010 ready-to-wear collection (figs 4a, 5a). The influence of the headdresses of Stefanoviki and Astypalaia is plainly visible in figs 4a and 5a, respectively. Photos: John Galliano Archives, Autumn-Winter 2009-2010. style.com

Side by side with Galliano's creations are the headdresses worn with the local costumes of Stefanoviki (fig. 4b) and Astypalaia (fig. 5b). Peloponnesian Folklore Foundation Collection, Nafplio

exemplify the possibilities offered by Greek local costume as a physical object, in terms of form, materials and decoration. The foreign press hailed this Galliano collection as 'costume design worthy of a far more elaborate stage' (Jones 2009), and Ioanna Papantoniou commented, 'The collection is notable for its incredible dynamism, which ought to be the envy of our own designers.' (Papantoniou 2010: 25).

Greek local costumes have also inspired designs for the theatre and the cinema. Numerous examples could be cited, not only in the modern Greek theatrical repertoire, where the 'folk' element is integrated into the narrative – as in *Babylonia* by Dimitrios Vyzantios – but also in ancient Greek drama, in the contemporary international repertoire and in musical theatre and opera (Pantouvaki 2013). The big difference between fashion design and performance costume design lies in the fact that a theatrical costume always functions within the context of a production; in other words, it is created for a specific play and can only be interpreted in the context of that play. This means that one and the same garment can have different meanings in different contexts. The use of features taken from local costumes in theatrical costume design is always connected with the aesthetic and conceptual codes of the production, in such a way that the 'folk' element is transmuted into an expressive medium.

Two stage and costume designers, in particular, epitomise in their artistic work the multifarious potential of local costume when used in designing a performance: Yorgos Ziakas and Ioanna Papantoniou. Both are former members of folk-dance companies and have spent many years doing research on popular culture. These are the two factors that have had a decisive bearing on their in-depth research into folk costumes and the incorporation of selected features of those costumes in a creative dialogue with their various stage directors. Ziakas' costumes based on Greek local costumes are to be found chiefly in his designs for ancient Greek drama. For example, for Euripides' *Electra* (Municipal and Regional Theatre of Larissa [MRTL] – Thessalian Theatre, 1988), he had the young women of the chorus dressed in black outfits based on the Karagouna's winter costume, while Electra, played by Lydia Koniordou, wore an under-chemise exactly like that of the Tanagra local costume (fig. 6). In Euripides' *Iphigenia in Tauris* (MRTL – Thessalian Theatre, 1990), he made use of folk decorative motifs done in gold embroidery on a black ground. In *The Libation Bearers* (*Choephoroi*) by Aeschylus (MRTL – Thessalian Theatre, 1992), Ioanna Papantoniou, as costume designer, gave Clytemnestra the striking headdress shown in the lithograph by Louis Dupré entitled *Mariage grec à Athènes* (see p. 208) combined with an imposing *doulamás*. Papantoniou also used elements of local costumes in plays of the international repertoire: in Lorca's *Yerma* (National Theatre of Greece, 1999-2000), the women's costumes were cut in the shape of the sleeveless Western-style dress of Trikeri, as they were again in Brecht's *The Caucasian Chalk Circle* (National Theatre of Greece, 2005). Papantoniou's costume designs for the opera *The Chessboard Fugitives* by Giorgos Kouroupos and Evgenios Trivizas (Greek National Opera, 1998-1999) were another special case: here, one can see any number of elements drawn from local costumes or other, older forms of dress, such as the garments worn by the dragomans of the Ottoman period used in the costumes for the kings in the opera (fig. 7).

Other stage and costume designers also turned to local costumes in search of dress forms, symbolic meanings and decorative designs in specific cases: for example, Yorgos Asimakopoulos (Aristophanes, *The Frogs*, National Theatre of Greece, 1998), Rena Georgiadou (Aristophanes, *Lysistrata*, National Theatre of Greece, 2004) and

Fig. 6. Lydia Koniordou as Electra. Costume by Yorgos Ziakas. Photo from the MRTL – Thessalian Theatre production of Euripides' *Electra*, 1988. Photo: Vassilis Agglopoulos. Municipal and Regional Theatre of Larissa Photographic Archive, Larissa

Fig. 7. Working drawings by Ioanna Papantoniou for the costumes of the King and Queen, for the opera *The Chessboard Fugitives* by Giorgos Kouroupos and Evgenios Trivizas. Greek National Opera, 1998-1999. Sofia Pantouvaki Collection

Fig. 8. Garment inspired by the
foustanella, created in the context
of the research project
The Forgotten Peacock, which set out
to redefine the men's jacket.
Takis, 'Plus' collection, 2008.
Photo: Grace Vane Percy.
Takis Archive

Yiannis Katranitsas, who, for the costume of Tassos in both versions of the modern adaptation of the late 19th-century dramatic romance *Golfo* by Spyridon Peresiadis (Iloros Theatre Company, Athens, 2004, 2005-2007), combined a simplified form of foustanella – completely divorced from its roots in traditional local culture – with the style of Japanese manga comics (Konstantinakou 2013).

Greek local costumes continue to inspire younger generations. The Greek performance and costume designer Takis, who works in London, included the foustanella among the sources of inspiration he used for his fashion and costume research project, *The Forgotten Peacock*. As a result, he created the garment which he named '+D07' for his 'Plus' collection (fig. 8), which explores the idea of adornment in contemporary men's fashion.

Somewhere between the Greek 'traditional fashion' of the mid-20th century and the 'new tradition of Greek fashion' of the second half of the 20th century, the designers of today will have to decide whether they are interested in creating a 'new fashion' by taking a fresh look at the Greek tradition from the viewpoint of the 21st century. The first examples mentioned above point to a contemporary creative trend that is making headway: a trend characterised by a polyphonic approach and multi-level readings of the potential offered by Greek local costumes. Moving on from the 'folklore' approach and the 'ethnic' approach, a deeper and more constructive – and also more personal – study of the aesthetic and morphological elements of local costumes could perhaps lay a firm foundation for interpreting those elements and turning them into a source of inspiration for future fashion and costume designs.

I am most grateful to my friend Vassilis Christodoulou and to Mrs Christiana Christodoulou, Cultural Adviser at the Laiki Bank Cultural Centre, for the loan of the exhibition catalogue *Beyond Dress Codes: From Traditional Costume to Contemporary Fashion*.

Women's Fashion in England:
The Influence of Ancient Greek Dress
on the Dress Reform Movement of the Late 19th Century

Myrsini Pichou

Variety and complexity are two of the characteristic features of traditional Greek costumes, and one can only wonder at the processes whereby, over the centuries, the peplos and chiton were superseded by costumes that evolved from the Byzantine tradition (Papantoniou 1996: 12). In the traditional forms of dress surviving from the 18th and 19th centuries, it is hard to see any connection with antiquity, though in some of them it is possible to discern features that may have been patterned on ancient clothing. Indicatively, Ioanna Papantoniou speculated that dresses from Crete reflect the influence of the Ionic chiton (Papantoniou 2000: 166-170). She also noted that in the early 19th-century chemises of Kassos and Karpathos (see p. 82) the form of the dalmatic 'coexists with the *kolpos* of the chiton' (Papantoniou 2000: 118).

Unlike traditional costumes, whose influence on contemporary designers was less marked or less well known,[1] ancient Greek costume exerted considerable power on the evolution of Western fashion. The admiration for the Greco-Roman world that played such an important part in the evolution of Western art and architecture was apparent in the field of fashion, too. In the early and late 19th century, women's dress in England was inspired by ancient Greek costume. In the early decades of the 19th century, that was the prevailing fashion trend, and it reappeared in the closing decades; and then, even though it did not carry the day, it played a part in the subsequent major reappraisal of the significance of fashion.

In post-revolutionary France, unlike England, the Greco-Roman model had an impact on all the arts, including dress. It was then that the Directoire style came into being, followed soon after by the Empire style. In these styles, which bore signs of the influence of ancient forms of dress, the changing shape of the female silhouette finally crystallised, with a high waist, lightweight materials and a simpler outline. As Lydia Kamitsis has pointed out, 'The garments of this period, which proceeded from the dressmaker's technique of their day, are objectively at the opposite extreme to the dress system of the ancient world, which was based on draping a rectangular piece of fabric.' (Kamitsis 2004: 81). This fashion was widely adopted in England, but there it remained less true to the original, for it was tinged with more Romantic overtones. Ancient Greek garments became points of reference once again in the closing decades of the 19th century, when, in the context of the Dress Reform Movement in women's fashions – 'the first real anti-

Fig. 1. A contemporary cartoon:
'The Venus of Milo; or, Girls of Two Different Periods.'
'Chorus: 'Look at her Big Foot! Oh, What a Waist! –
and what a Ridiculous Little Head! –
and *no* Chignon! She's no Lady! Oh, what a Fright!'
Artist: DM. From the *Punch Almanack* for 1870.
Gennadius Library – The American School of Classical Studies at Athens

HE VENUS OF MILO; OR, GIRLS OF TWO DIFFERENT PERIODS.

fashion for women' (Ribeiro 2003: 119) – it was presented as one of the counter-proposals to the fashion then prevailing.

From the middle of the 19th century, in Victorian England,[2] there developed a new and more widespread interest in ancient Greece, involving artists, scientists, scholars and intellectuals. The achievements of ancient Greek civilisation were widely known, due to classical education, and were further publicised through the new archaeological discoveries that aroused the Victorians' admiration (Challis 2012). In particular, the Parthenon sculptures (on public view at the British Museum from 1817) provided fertile ground for artistic inspiration, which received a further boost when they were redisplayed in the 1860s. There was a general feeling of familiarity with ancient Greece: 'Victorian England, at the height of its prosperity and political supremacy, came to see itself as a modern inheritor of the Hellenic values [...]' (Evangelista 2009: 9). All these factors led to the use of designs based on ancient garments in an effort to reform women's clothes.

From the mid-19th century, with the help of industrialisation, fashion started changing at a faster rate than before and became more complex. Its dictates, which came from Paris and were aimed at a wider public, called for a multi-part outfit with any number of accessories, which were constantly being changed in accordance with the rules of etiquette. In the same period, especially after 1870, the fashion world came under heavy fire both for its irrationality and for its questionable taste, while there was no denying the 'lack of resemblance to the clothing of the Greeks' (Newton 1974: 42).

The deformed female silhouette and the voluminous hairstyles, the narrow, high-heeled shoes and the tightly laced corsets – all the features dictated by fashion – were widely discussed and satirised (fig. 1). Moreover, these protestations were fuelled by the arguments of the medical profession against the tight lacing of the corset, which caused permanent damage to the human frame, respiratory problems and difficulties for women in childbirth. The opponents of the current fashion – members of the intellectual and social élite – could see that it was far removed, both in construction and in taste, from the simplicity and practicality of ancient Greek clothing. They argued that it distorted the natural shape and beauty of the female body as exemplified by the *Venus de Milo*, which embodied the ideal beauty so admired by the Victorians, especially in artistic circles.

The solution to the problem was dress reform. The advocates of rational dress propounded arguments against a fashion that restricted movement and was bad for the health. In 1881 the Rational Dress Society[3] was formed, and an article in an 1888 issue of its *Gazette* explained how, by the study of the sculptures and pottery in the British Museum, 'one comes to understand by what simple and perfect appliance the logical Greek mind arrived at results in harmony with then existing conditions' (Burman Baines 1981: 48). The Society's members were intent on the adoption of a healthier and more practical form of dress, which, just like ancient clothing, could be adapted to contemporary needs. This was the period when women were fighting for emancipation and their rights, for they were now spending more of their time outside the house, taking part in sports and, in some cases, working.

At the same time, the artists and intellectuals of the Aesthetic Movement[4] denounced contemporary fashion for its dependence on industrial production. They went back to the pre-industrial past in search of a model, a source of inspiration, for the recovery of the lost beauty of clothing; and eventually they put forward a proposal for an 'artistic' or 'aesthetic' form of dress. They invested clothing with the properties of a work of art; and they made it a fundamental part of their effort to introduce beauty into every aspect of life (Stern 2004: 9).

By about the middle of the 19th century a garment had been designed which was worn by the women who were the artists' muses: it was similar to the dresses depicted in the paintings of the Pre-Raphaelite Brotherhood and reflected the influence of the Middle Ages. This early, *timeless* Aesthetic dress was more comfortable, more flowing, with voluminous folds; it did away with the corset and crinoline, placed the waist at its natural height and had comfortably wide sleeves. Its sequel, the more elaborate Aesthetic dress, borrowed features (often in combination) from Greco-Roman times, the Middle Ages, the Renaissance, the 18th century and the archaising fashions of the early 19th century, since the dominant idea of the Aesthetic Movement was 'a belief that anything old was bound to be better' (Ormond 1968: 34). An attitude common to the advocates of Aesthetic and rational dress in the late 19th century was their admiration for ancient Greek clothing, which was simpler, 'unfussy' and classic, while at the same time showing the natural curves of the body without either distorting or constricting them.

What the Victorians had to achieve was to adapt ancient dress to their own era. According to one critic, 'It would be more possible to disestablish the Church, abolish the House of Lords, and cut the sacred vesture of the British Constitution into little pieces, than to translate English garments into Greek.' (Oliphant 1878: 68). At the same time, though, in conformity with their moral code, the Victorians were against the adoption of anything suggestive of ancient Greek dress, since it was associated with exposure of the body – which meant that it could not be worn by 'nations who have lost to a great extent the simple instinct of natural beauty, whilst they have grown abnormally self-conscious and reflective' (Haweis 1883: 26). As Oscar Wilde wrote in 1884, a solution could be reached with a modernised style; however, he added that he was 'not proposing any antiquarian revival of ancient costume, but trying merely to point out the right laws of dress, laws which are dictated by art and not by archaeology, by science and not by fashion' (Stern 2004: 114). The fundamental concepts of ancient Greek dress might be perfectly realised, he contended, in 'the principle of suspending all apparel from the shoulders, and of relying for beauty of effect not on the stiff ready-made ornaments of the modern milliner [...] but on the exquisite play of light and line that one gets from rich and rippling folds'. The folds so characteristic of ancient dress – as preserved in the finds surviving from the ancient era and particularly as rendered in idealised form in ancient sculpture – were an inseparable and common element in the Victorians' admiration for the ancient sartorial model.

The finds from ancient Greece in the British Museum exerted a powerful influence on 19th-century artists and scholars; and at the same time they offered material for the study of the original ancient Greek style and were a source of inspiration for 'classical' creative works. Ideas for points of detail or for antique dress designs, without corsets and in a variety of bold colours, could be gleaned from paintings on Greek and Roman subjects by such contemporary artists as Albert Moore, Frederic Leighton and Lawrence Alma-Tadema. The classicising trend of Aesthetic dress followed and was influenced by the appearance of Greek and Roman subjects in art, while the opulence and pleasure-loving disposition of the people depicted in those paintings were reflected in the rendering of the clothes, especially the folds.

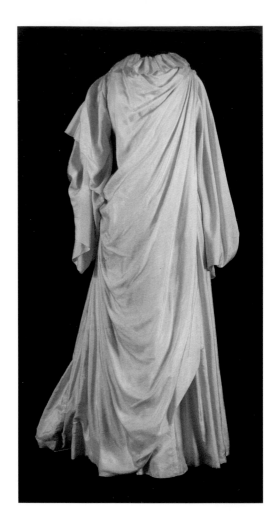

"HERMIONE."

A graceful COSTUME, adapted from the Greek, for Evening wear or as a Tea Gown. The bands and bottom of Dress hand-embroidered.

Fig.2. The wedding dress worn by Geraldine Southall at her marriage to Barrow Cadbury in 1891. Made by Liberty & Co., London. The dress, of white silk with a cotton lining, has a fitted inner bodice and a long, lacy train behind.
Birmingham Museum & Art Gallery

Fig. 3. The 'Hermione' gown, suggested as an evening dress or a tea gown. From the 1894 catalogue *'Liberty' Costumes, Mantles and Millinery for Ladies and Children, Season 1894-5.*
National Art Library, Victoria and Albert Museum, London

In 1884, Liberty & Co. in London opened a Costume Department with its own atelier, under the supervision of the architect and designer Edward William Godwin. Since its foundation in 1875, Liberty's had developed into a major centre for the promotion and cultivation of 'Aesthetic' taste, bringing fabrics and other merchandise in the 'Aesthetic' style to a wider public. In the Costume Department customers could choose to order one of the available models or to create their own attire. One outfit bearing the Liberty's label is the wedding dress worn by Geraldine Southall at her marriage to Barrow Cadbury in 1891 (fig. 2). One of the striking features of this silk gown, in which the combined influence of several historical periods is apparent, is the antiquarian, 'Aesthetic' way the drapery is thrown over the left shoulder and wrapped round the body, recalling the ancient himation

In popular handbooks and in the catalogues of Liberty's Costume Department, amongst the creations incorporating features reminiscent of various historical periods there also some classical designs. These gowns, bearing such appropriate names as 'Andromeda', 'Hermione' (fig. 3) and 'Hera', were sometimes closer to their ancient models and sometimes harked back to the classical revival of the early 19th century, while incorporating other historical elements as well. One of the most popular, the 'Hera' dress,[5] was intended to be worn either as an evening dress or as a tea gown, and variants of it continued to be worn for many years (fig. 4).

The tea gown, a more casual dress worn for afternoon tea or at gatherings of family and friends at home, made its appearance in the 1870s and became immensely popular.[6] As less constricting and being informal, worn infrequently in public, it was not required to conform to the last word in fashion; and so it offered every woman – even the most conservative lady who did not move in artistic circles – an ideal canvas for 'Aesthetic' touches, which helped to boost its popularity.

However, the more avant-garde Aesthetic costumes – as well as the aesthetes' way of life – were considered outlandish by people who did not belong to artistic circles and were savagely lampooned. The sort of impression made by an Aesthetic dress in its purest form on the Victorian beholder is described in the satirical novel *Miss Brown*, published in 1884: 'It was of that Cretan silk, not much thicker than muslin, which is woven in minute wrinkles of palest yellowy white; [...] more like a night-gown than anything else, shapeless and yet clinging with large and small folds, and creases like those of damp

Fig 4. Olive Crofton (née Schneider),
Lady Smith–Dorrien, wearing a 'Hera'
gown, 3 May 1911.
Photo: Bassano Ltd.
National Portrait Gallery, London

sculptor's drapery, or the garments of Mantegna's women [...] in half-antique, half-medieval guise' (Lee 1884: 306, 307). Even so, antique, Aesthetic outfits gained steadily in popularity, so much so that in 1885 the Royal Academy in London gave a reception to which the ladies were asked 'to come dressed as Grecian damsels' (Jenkyns 1980: 301).

The forces of reform advocating rational and Aesthetic attire became formally allied in 1890 with the foundation of the Healthy and Artistic Dress Union.[7] The Union's ideological platform and the proposals of its members were set out at length in its journal, *Aglaia*.[8] It was in *Aglaia*, too, that an advertisement appeared for the 'Athenian' gown (fig. 5), made of French crépon, designed for wear as an evening dress or tea gown: although this garment made use of a blend of elements from different periods, its distinctive decorative motif was the meander, which gave it the required 'antique' look.

Early in the 20th century, the Spanish artist and designer Mariano Fortuny, who was acquainted with the reformers' efforts and was himself influenced by ancient Greece, created in his Venetian palazzo the most popular 'antique' gown in the history of fashion (fig. 6), in which 'he invented rather than replicated a Hellenic style' (Koda 2003: 167). In acknowledgement of the influence of the *Charioteer of Delphi* with a pleated chiton, this dress, similarly pleated, came to be known as the 'Delphos' gown. It was designed to be a comfortable garment to be worn without a corset and signalled such a marked break with established principles that it was worn as a tea gown, as well as by a few progressive women, mostly from the art world. For its construction in 1907 Fortuny devised a ground-breaking method of holding the pleats in place, which he patented in 1909. Having succeeded in 'ensuring that he would be frustrated by neither fashion nor convention' (de Osma 1980: 95), he produced several variations on the 'Delphos' between 1907 and his death in 1949, in a variety of hues. Taking his cue from ancient clothing, Fortuny realised the dream of the Victorian reformers, for he created a practical, lightweight garment that showed the natural proportions of the body to good advantage and established itself as a benchmark in the history of fashion, thanks to its timelessness and the brilliance of its construction.

Although the dress reformers in Victorian England did not actually succeed in changing the fashion of their time, they did help to set in motion a re-examination of its substance and significance. They took ancient dress as their model because it went against the dress code of their time (Pichou 2009: 35); and they hailed it as ideal for the harmony of its simplicity, its enduring beauty and the freedom it gave to the female body, which it released from the 'straitjacket' of the corset. Moreover, not only was the adoption of the ancient Greek model well suited to provide an Aesthetic alternative or a rational dress solution, but it expressed an ideal connected with the perception of the natural perfection of the Greek body, as portrayed in ancient Greek sculpture (Challis 2012: 55).

Given that one of the reformers' fundamental tenets was 'that the attire shall express to a reasonable extent the character of the wearer' (Haweis 1883: 23), they maintained that

Fig. 5. An advertisement for the 'Athenian' gown from Capper, Son & Co. Ltd in *Aglaia: The Journal of the Healthy and Artistic Dress Union*. Autumn 1894.
National Art Library, Victoria and Albert Museum, London

Fig. 6. 'Peplos' gown by Mariano Fortuny, a variation of the 'Delphos', of pleated mauve silk. 1910–1920. Gloria Vanderbilt Collection, Italy. Peloponnesian Folklore Foundation, Nafplio

clothes were connected with personal identity and personal choice, thus legitimising the idea of difference. To that extent, Aesthetic dress came to be the prevailing fashion trend for women who moved in intellectual and artistic circles.

Towards the end of the 19th century, those ladies who chose to wear archaising, Aesthetic dress felt that they were escaping from the restrictions of contemporary fashion and creating their own dress conventions. This property of Aesthetic dress eventually helped to bring about a change in the sartorial status quo in the 20th century (Cunningham 2002: 214): the use of the ancient Greco-Roman model and the efforts of the reformers influenced later designers, such as Mariano Fortuny and Paul Poiret, promoting the creation of classical revivals in fashion[9] and opening the way to the simplification of women's dress styles in the 20th century.

NOTES

1. See the related essay herein.

2. Queen Victoria reigned from 1837 to 1901.

3. One of its founder members, and its President, was Florence Wallace Pomeroy, Lady Harberton, a champion of the emancipation of women.

4. Among the intellectuals and artists associated with the Aesthetic Movement were the writer Oscar Wilde, the illustrator Aubrey Beardsley, the artists James Abbott McNeill Whistler, Dante Gabriel Rossetti, Albert Moore, Frederic Leighton, George Frederic Watts and Edward Burne-Jones, and the architect and designer Edward William Godwin.

5. An example of the 'Hera' dress (1905–1909) is to be found in the Gallery of Costume in Platt Hall, Manchester.

6. The tea gown, which needed no corset, was an alternative to stiff formal dress and was designed to allow greater freedom of movement.

7. Its founder members included the artist George Frederic Watts and his wife, Mary Seton Fraser Tytler, the painter Louise Jopling and Lady Muncaster, among other representatives of the *beau monde*.

8. The Three Graces of Greek mythology were Aglaia, Euphrosyne and Thalia, goddesses of beauty and grace.

9. Such as the revival of 'antique' fashion in the early 20th century, before the start of World War I.

Catalogue

1

Cotton dress

Karpathos, Dodecanese. 18th century
H. 1.405 m
Benaki Museum, Athens
EE 923

This dress is in the form of a dalmatic, with a large internal pleat, or overfold, resembling the *kolpos* of the ancient Greek chiton. It is embroidered with terracotta and green floss silk, using a stitch that Angeliki Hatzimichali called 'Rhodian'.

A similar dress from Kassos, an island near Karpathos in the Dodecanese, is depicted in the engraving *Femme de l'isle de Cassos* (Woman from Kassos) of 1825 (fig. 1). The book in which it was published was based on drawings done by Otto Magnus von Stackelberg (1786-1837) in the course of his tour of Greece in 1811. Von Stackelberg devoted his life to the arts and archaeology.

The dotted line on the pattern of a dress from Kassos (fig. 2) marks the position of the overfold.

Fig. 1. Otto Magnus von Stackelberg,
Femme de l'isle de Cassos **(Woman from Kassos [Dodecanese]),**
hand-coloured copper engraving, 36 x 24 cm.
From his book *Costumes et usages des peuples de la Grèce moderne,* **Rome 1825.**
Alpha Bank Photographic Archive, Athens

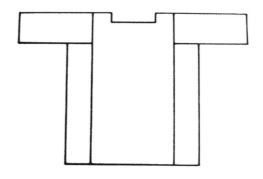

Fig. 2. Pattern of a dress from Kassos, Dodecanese.
Peloponnesian Folklore Foundation Archive, Nafplio

2

Samaráki, a short red cotton dress

Mesta, Chios, North-East Aegean Islands. Early 20th century
H. 0.42 m
Peloponnesian Folklore Foundation, Nafplio
1990.6.57

Note the tight pleating on the back and the multicoloured brocade applied at the nape of the neck. The straight opening at the front is laced up. This *samaráki* belonged to the Yialouris family.

The costume of Mesta, Chios (the *bambazína*), as worn in the early 20th century, comprises an inner chemise, a pleated skirt of fine calico with narrow pleats and appliqué braids on the hem, and a second, short chemise of finer material (cotton or silk) with decorative designs round the armholes and cuffs. Over those is the *samaráki*, a dress so short as to be hardly more than a bodice. The rather inelegant front opening is covered by two *stithópana* (chest kerchiefs): one large one of fine white calico, embroidered round the perimeter, and another made from a coloured kerchief or from an oblong piece of brocade. The hair is parted in the middle and covered with a cap of fine white calico, with a ringlet hanging down on each side. Over the cap is a triangular kerchief, of fine white calico, with a very long (about five metres) silk *bólia*, the *bambazína*, wound round it and knotted at the back of the head so that the embroidered ends are visible. The whole headdress is adorned at the back with multicoloured *karkavelónes* and finished off with a wreath of multicoloured artificial flowers. Knee-length knitted openwork white cotton stockings are worn inside *yemeniá* or ordinary shoes.

An older form of the Mesta costume is depicted in the engraving *Femme de l'isle de Chios* (Woman from Chios) of 1825 (fig. 3), after the drawing by Otto Magnus von Stackelberg (see cat. no. 1).

Fig. 3. Otto Magnus von Stackelberg,
Femme de l'isle de Chios **(Woman from Chios**
[North-East Aegean Islands]),
hand-coloured copper engraving, 36 x 24 cm.
From his book *Costumes et usages des peuples de la Grèce moderne*, **Rome 1825.**
Alpha Bank Photographic Archive, Athens

3

Pleated cotton dress
Crete. 18th century
H. 1.387 m
Benaki Museum, Athens
EE 871

This is a simpler variation of the Cretan dresses with their magnificent embroidered hems. Cretan dresses are literally suspended from the shoulders by shoulder straps. Some travellers' accounts imply that the women of Sfakia wore them with no chemise, leaving the shoulders bare.

The engraving *Candiotes* (Women of Crete) of 1817 (fig. 4) comes from the book by Joseph Pitton de Tournefort (1656-1708), a renowned physician and botanist of his day, describing his travels in the Near East in the early 18th century. It shows two women wearing long dresses. One of the dresses hangs loosely from the shoulders; the other only comes up to just below the bust. The two horizontal lines at about knee height may be pleats indicating the position of the hem. Under the dress, each of the women is wearing a very wide-sleeved chemise, which may also be considered a simpler variant of the Cretan dresses. (See also the pattern of a Cretan dress, fig. 5.)

The Cretan dress in the Benaki Museum has two bands of red silk embroidery on the hem: one with floral designs, running parallel to the hem, and another above it with vases of flowers alternating with cross-in-circle motifs.

Fig. 4. *Candiotes* (Women of Crete),
copper engraving, 18.5 x 12 cm.
From Joseph Pitton de Tournefort,
Relation d'un voyage du Levant, Paris 1717.
Peloponnesian Folklore Foundation, Nafplio
Donated by Ioanna Papantoniou

Fig. 5. Pattern of a Cretan dress.
Peloponnesian Folklore Foundation
Archive, Nafplio

4

Part of the hem of a Cretan dress
Crete. 18th century
0.71 x 0.40 m
Peloponnesian Folklore Foundation, Nafplio
Donated by Ioanna Papantoniou
1976.7.39

The hem, made of off-white linen, is richly decorated with multicoloured embroidered flowers, animals and a mermaid. (See also the hem embroidery, cat. no. 3.)

The embroideries are taken from Venetian lace designs. The nuns of the Catholic convents on the Greek Islands taught women to make lace, which they then shipped to the West. According to Popi Zora, Greek women often copied these lace designs in their embroideries.

5

Phelonion made of a linen-cotton fabric, with multicoloured silk embroidery

Crete. Late 18th century
H. 1.50 m
Peloponnesian Folklore Foundation, Nafplio
1976.7.40

An 18th-century Cretan dress remade as a church vestment (see also cat. no. 6).

6

Phelonion made of a linen-cotton fabric, with openwork embroidery

Crete. Late 18th century
H. 1.30 m
Peloponnesian Folklore Foundation, Nafplio
Donated by Ioanna Papantoniou
2009.6.812

An 18th-century Cretan dress remade as a church vestment (see also cat. no. 5).

7

White linen chemise
Trikeri, Magnesia, Thessaly. Early 20th century
H. 1.28 m
Peloponnesian Folklore Foundation, Nafplio
Donated by Ioanna Papantoniou
1976.6.517

The chemise is decorated with multicoloured floral embroideries on the sleeves and cockerels on the hem (see also cat. no. 8).

The chemise of Greek local costumes is derived from the dalmatic (fig. 6). The garment forms that became standard in the Early Christian period in the Mediterranean countries were based on the dalmatic, which had evolved from the Roman *tunica*. The dalmatic is made up from more than one piece of cloth. The main part is a long, wide, rectangular strip of cloth hanging down at the front and back, with an opening in the centre for the head. Sleeves are sewn on to this, and additional gussets are let into the side seams, allowing the garment to fit the shape of the body to some extent without narrowing at the hem. This garment lived on for many centuries in Greek local costumes and is known as a *poukámiso*. Naturally enough, the dalmatic evolved differently in the East and the West. In the East, after the fall of Constantinople in 1453, garments based on the dalmatic and the *tunica* became almost 'set in stone' and were confused with Eastern garments of similar cut.

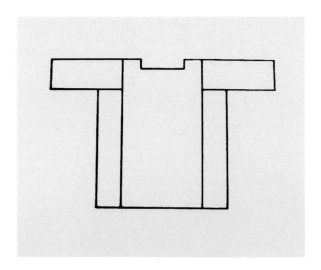

**Fig. 6. Pattern of a dalmatic.
Peloponnesian Folklore Foundation Archive,
Nafplio**

8

Geránio, blue linen chemise
Trikeri, Magnesia, Thessaly. Early 20th century
H. 1.30 m
Peloponnesian Folklore Foundation, Nafplio
Donated by M. Hart
1976.6.531

This chemise has multicoloured floral embroideries on the hem and cockerels on the sleeves (see also cat. no. 7).

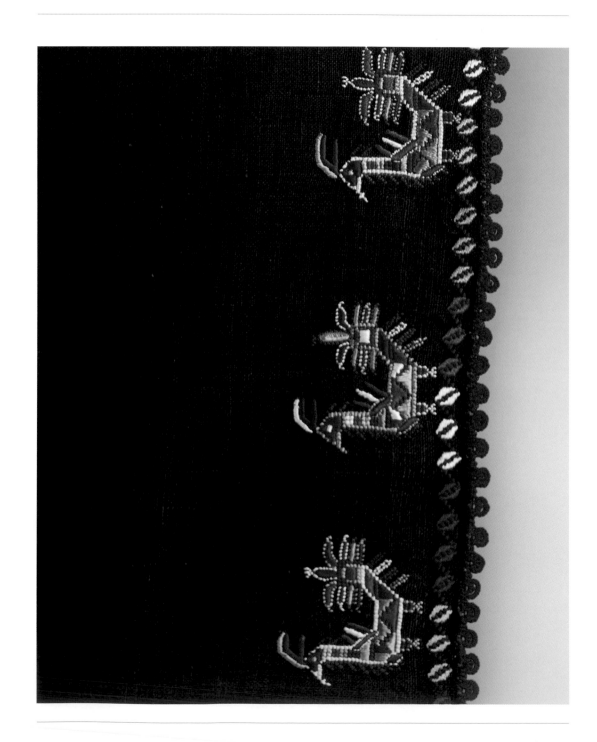

9

Linomániko, Karagouna costume chemise
Thessaly. Early 20th century
H. 1.2 m
Peloponnesian Folklore Foundation, Nafplio
Donated by Ioanna Papantoniou
1976.6.633

The *linomániko* of the Karagouna costume is made of beige linen, with long sleeves, upright collar and a neck opening at the front. It is embroidered with geometric designs in black, crimson, green and blue, with silk thread. There are red and black tassels on the sleeves and black tassels on the hem.

The bridal or festive costume worn by the Karagounes (fig. 7) of the Thessalian plain comprises the *linomániko* chemise and two richly pleated cotton coat dresses, the *sayádes*. The outer *sayás* is usually indigo in colour and has an appliqué embroidered hem, which matches the waistcoat, embroidered by specialist tailors using multicoloured fine cords. The chest is covered by a cotton dickey. The costume is completed by a felt apron and the *kavadománika*, again embroidered by a specialist tailor using multicoloured or gold cords. The head is covered by a black cotton or silk kerchief made up in an unusual shape, and thick tresses of faux hair are attached at the back. A great deal of jewellery, mostly chains with coins, is worn on the head, the chest, the waist and the apron. Small locks of the wearer's own hair are often left peeping out from under the headdress on the cheeks: these are called *ramónes*.

Fig. 7. Photo of a Karagouna from Trikala, Thessaly. Early 20th century. Benaki Museum Photographic Archive, Athens

10

Sleeveless, off-white cotton chemise
Mesogeia region, Attica. Early 20th century
H. 1.35 m
Peloponnesian Folklore Foundation, Nafplio
Donated by Ioanna Papantoniou
1976.6.625

This chemise, typical of the costume of Attica (figs 8, 9, 35), has a vertical opening at the front and is decorated on the hem with multicoloured embroideries of geometric motifs.

Fig. 8. Postcard of a woman wearing a costume of Attica. Early 20th century. Peloponnesian Folklore Foundation, Nafplio
Donated by Ioanna Papantoniou

Fig. 9. Otto Magnus von Stackelberg, *Paysanne des environs d'Athènes en habit de fête* (Village woman from the vicinity of Athens in festive costume), hand-coloured copper engraving, 26 x 20 cm. From his book *Costumes et usages des peuples de la Grèce moderne*, Rome 1825.
Alpha Bank Photographic Archive, Athens

11

Long-sleeved, off-white cotton chemise

Stymphalia, Corinthia, Peloponnese. Late 19th century
H. 1.28 m
Peloponnesian Folklore Foundation, Nafplio
Donated by Ioanna Papantoniou
1976.6.1155

The chemise has a vertical opening at the front and is decorated with multicoloured silk embroideries of geometric motifs and with added-on triangles on the sleeves (see also cat nos 12, 13).

This chemise is part of the old-style type of village women's costume of Corinthia, the Argolid and probably the whole Peloponnese. The village costume is always made up of the same items, but with different decorative embroideries on all parts of it. It consists of a plain inner chemise and an embroidered outer one, a short-sleeved fitted bodice with the sleeves embroidered all over, the *dzákos*, a white sleeveless woollen outer garment of varying length, and a *sigoúni* girdled with a red *zóstra*, which is made of sprang mesh, with long fringes at both ends. The *zóstra* was worn low down on the waist to support the abdomen during pregnancy. For the wedding itself, the bride's chest was covered by a dickey with all-over embroidery, and her belly by a special protective apron. Her hair was parted in the centre and braided into two plaits hanging down the back, which were adorned with special crimson tasselled cords and enlaced silver ornaments, the *kremastária* or *piskoúlia*. Her head was swathed in a *messáli*, a coarsely woven *bólia* with

double-sided embroideries at the ends and fringes. Women used to knot the *messáli* into the shape of a cross, which the master builder would embed in the roof of their house; then, when the house was built, he would take it out and wear it on his head.

The picture of the woman wearing the characteristic costume of Stymphalia, Corinthia (fig. 10), dates from the early 20th century.

Fig. 10. Postcard of a woman wearing a costume of Stymphalia, Corinthia, Peloponnese. Early 20th century. Peloponnesian Folklore Foundation, Nafplio Donated by Ioanna Papantoniou

12

Kolonáto, a long-sleeved, off-white cotton chemise

Stymphalia, Corinthia, Peloponnese. Late 19th century
H. 1.25 m
Peloponnesian Folklore Foundation, Nafplio
Donated by Ioanna Papantoniou
1976.6.1150

The *kolonáto* chemise, found in the Peloponnese, has embroideries arranged in columns (*kolónes*). This particular *kolonáto* from Stymphalia is open at the neck and is decorated with multicoloured silk embroideries of geometric designs on the sleeves and plant motifs on the hem (fig. 11; see also cat. nos 11, 13).

The painter and lithographer Théodore Leblanc (1800-1837), who spent some time in Greece during the 1820s, drew, amongst others, a country woman in the Peloponnese wearing the traditional local costume (fig. 11).

Fig. 11. Théodore Leblanc, *Femme Vlagne (Morée)*
(Country woman [the Morea]),
hand-coloured lithograph, 31 x 22 cm.
From the album *Croquis d'après nature faits pendant trois
***ans de séjour en Grèce et dans le Levant*, Paris 1833-1834.**
Peloponnesian Folklore Foundation, Nafplio
Donated by Ioanna Papantoniou

13

Long-sleeved, off-white cotton chemise
Stymphalia, Corinthia, Peloponnese. Early 20th century
H. 1.30 m
Peloponnesian Folklore Foundation, Nafplio
Donated by Ioanna Papantoniou
1976.6.1149

The chemise has a vertical opening at the front and an embroidered sewn-over bib. It is decorated with multicoloured silk embroideries of geometric motifs, while the sleeves have added-on triangles (see also cat. nos 11, 12).

14

Off-white bridal chemise
Episkopi, Imathia, Macedonia. Early 20th century
H. 1.29 m
Peloponnesian Folklore Foundation, Nafplio
Donated by Ioanna Papantoniou
1990.6.507

This bridal chemise has a small upright collar, a vertical opening at the front and long, wide sleeves. The hem has four square panels embroidered with multicoloured geometric motifs and crosses.

The bridal costume of Episkopi (fig. 12) has the *fanéla* next to the skin, with ornamental sleeves sewn on, and a white cotton chemise. The hem of the chemise has four large ornamental square panels, two at the front and two at the back, embroidered with multicoloured silk and gold threads. Next come the *kavádi*, a long-sleeved overdress made of spotted crimson velvet, silken *taraklí* or some other luxury fabric, and the white or blue *sayás* with sleeves rolled up to the elbow to show the *bougasía* (the red lining). The two decorated inner parts of the *sayás* that show when the sleeves are rolled up are called the *póli*; in church, the sleeves are not turned back. Round the waist is a multicoloured woollen textile sash, folded diagonally, reinforced by the apron strings. The apron, or *diplári*, is short, almost square, with woven-in gold and multicoloured geometrical designs. Over that is a gold-embroidered velvet belt with silver buckles. The headdress, or *kalpáki*, worn only by married women, consists of a small kalpak (high-crowned cap) filled out at the base with padding, which is worn angled to one side (*lítsko*), with a

covering of fine red material, and held in place by the *trákma*, a gold-embroidered band to which plaits are fastened at the back. Over the kalpak and arranged in a distinctive way is a gold-embroidered white *tsembéri* fastened by special pins called *koumbouféles*. The costume is embellished with jewellery and ornaments of various kinds on the chest and the headdress. The knitted white stockings, called *tsourápia*, have toes and heels of a different colour.

Fig. 12. Photo of a woman wearing the bridal costume of Episkopi, Imathia, Macedonia. Early 20th century. Peloponnesian Folklore Foundation Photographic Archive, Nafplio

15

Bridal costume
Skopelos, Sporades. Early 20th century
Peloponnesian Folklore Foundation, Nafplio

The bridal costume of Skopelos is called *foustána* or *stófa* (fig. 13) after the long, richly pleated outer sleeveless dress, which is made of 16 metres of black silk satin. In earlier times it had a hem of brocade (*stófa*), which was later replaced by a band of lavish multicoloured embroidery with the same floral designs. There are four underdresses: the small and the large *f'stána* (a sort of crinoline), the *malakófi* and lastly the *kolovóli*, identical in shape to the outer *f'stána*. The *anetoráli* is a white silk chemise with gold lace and embroidery. The short velvet bodice is known as the *bambouklí* and its sleeves as *broumánika*: these are turned back to reveal the *timbadóxa* (the interior ornamentation). The *bambouklí* is usually held in place by the *kolaína*, a kind of small dickey, embroidered all over in gold, from which hangs the *tsatsaráki*, a short double ribbon, usually red or pale blue. The hair is worn in plaits, with loose strands forming curls (*dzouloúfia*) on the cheeks. The head is covered first with the *bounés*, a sort of snood made of black bouclé wool. Over that, on the crown, is the *kavoúki*, a kind of round cap, held on by a gold-embroidered chinstrap, the *chrysokap'tséli*, with the *sálpa*, an ornament of white satin and gold embroidery, attached on the right side. The *bounés* is covered by the *tsitsákia*, gold strings embellished with *tir-tir* (twisted gold foil) and spangles, with the ends hanging down on the right. On top of this there is a tulle headscarf, the *aéras*. This is the only costume in Greece that is worn with fingerless gloves, made of black or white lace. The footwear consists of knitted white openwork stockings and distinctive slippers called *kondoúres*

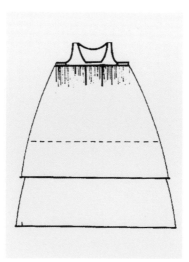

**Fig. 13. Pattern of a *foustána* (long, pleated, sleeveless dress),
part of the costume of Skopelos, Sporades.
Peloponnesian Folklore Foundation Archive, Nafplio**

16

Áspri vólta, a long, sleeveless, pleated dress
Skopelos, Sporades. Early 20th century
H. 1.21 m
Peloponnesian Folklore Foundation, Nafplio
Donated by Ioanna Papantoniou
1976.6.91

This particular dress, worn as an overdress or underdress, is made of fine white calico. Another type of dress from Skopelos, of the same period, is the *mórkos* (see cat. no. 17). Benjamin Mary (1792-1846), the Belgian chargé d'affaires at the court of King Otto, made a number of pencil drawings of girls wearing the Skopelos costume (fig. 14).

Fig. 14. Details from pencil drawings by Benjamin Mary
depicting girls wearing the Skopelos costume, 1840-1842.
From Benjamin Mary, *Νεοελληνισμού απαρχές.*
Προσωπογραφίες από την Ελλάδα του Όθωνα / La Grèce nouvelle. Portraits Grecs (1840-1844),
Lucy Braggiotti Editions, Athens 1992

17

Mórkos, a long, sleeveless, pleated dress
Skopelos, Sporades. Early 20th century
H. 1.26 m
Peloponnesian Folklore Foundation, Nafplio
Donated by Myrto Paraschi
1995.6.5

The dress is made of satin and has a red and green hem (see also cat. no. 16 and fig. 14).

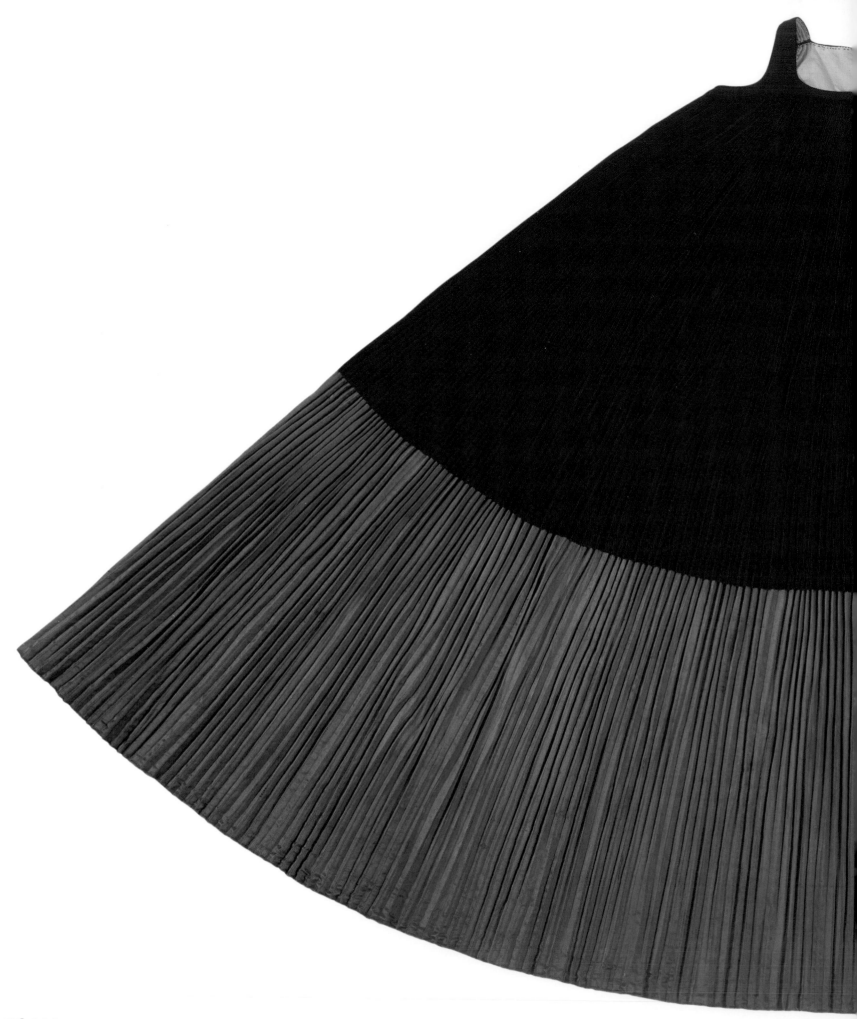

18

Bridal costume
Kymi, Euboea. 18th century
Peloponnesian Folklore Foundation, Nafplio

The bridal costume shown here is a real rarity. Typologically, it belongs among the island costumes of the Greek world, as these took shape in the 18th century.

The short chemise is of pure silk chequered material with delicate gold embroidery at the neck opening and round the sleeves. The dress, made of pure silk brocade imported from Europe, has a hem of a different brocade. The brocaded design of the hem is the same as that of the jacket, but the material is of poorer quality, which reveals the existence of two kinds of material with the same woven design. The jacket is made on the same pattern as the *gounéla* of the summer costume, with its dark, glossy *doúla foustáni*. Round the waist is a gold-embroidered belt with couched braid and *thilykotária* of hammered silver. The embroidery on the belt perfectly matches that of the mules, which are similar in shape to the *g'dóres* of Skyros. The mules are secured by two narrow, off-white silk ribbons tied in a bow round the ankle. The headdress consists of a white triangular *tsembéri* and a green triangular kerchief, wound into a sort of roll on one side. The part of it on the forehead is adorned with a large red 'moon' (*fengári*). A gossamer silk *bólia*, 3.25 metres long, covers the entire headdress; it has probably lost the gold trimming that is a usual feature of such scarves. The headdress is secured by a chinstrap, the *kapitsáli*, with embroidery matching that of the belt and mules.

Parts of the old-style costume can be found in combination with the costumes of later type.

19

Bridal costume
Trikeri, Magnesia, Thessaly. Early 20th century
Peloponnesian Folklore Foundation, Nafplio

The bridal costume of Trikeri has two fine white calico chemises and up to 13 petticoats, the main ones being the *kolovóli* and the *mallína*. The 'good' outermost chemise is made of linen or silk, in white, blue, crimson, brown or green, and is adorned with gold or multicoloured embroidery. The dress is richly pleated, sleeveless and short, and the hem is often ornamented. Round the waist is a very wide gold-embroidered belt fastened with large clasps, the *klidotária*. Tucked into the belt is a white or floral or gold-embroidered handkerchief, the *mandíli tou kórfou*. The costume includes two pieces of jewellery: the pectoral cross and the *kósses me ta klónia kai ta koumbiá*, which are silver ornaments for the plaits. (See the photograph by the pioneering Greek photographer Nelly's [1899-1998] of women from Trikeri wearing the local costume, fig. 15.)

Fig. 15. Women from Trikeri, Magnesia, Thessaly, wearing the local costume.
Photo: Nelly's. 1936.
Peloponnesian Folklore Foundation Photographic Archive, Nafplio

20

Bridal or festive costume
Skyros, Sporades. Early 20th century
Peloponnesian Folklore Foundation, Nafplio

The bridal *chrysí* or festive costume of Skyros consists of a petticoat, the *kolovóli*, a white embroidered under-chemise, a waistcoat of patterned brocade (*mendené*) and over these a second chemise, the *poukámiso me ta chrysá*, which is white from the waist down but has a crimson or green bodice of fine silk with gold embroidery. The embroidery on the *skoútes* (skirts) of both chemises is widely famed. Next comes the sleeveless dress (*kap'hás*), which is often made of rich brocade and has a decorative *poýdere* (hem). Over all these is a short sleeveless waistcoat, the *goúna*, with a buckled belt. The *podemí* (footwear) includes white knitted stockings with various patterns, as well as the *terlítsia* and *g'dóres*. The headdress consists of a *tsembéri* and, over it, a long white scarf (*bólia*) with a crimson central section, the *ópsi*. When the *bólia* has been passed over the head and the *ópsi* secured under the chin, the two embroidered ends hang gently to decorate the back. Over the *bólia* is the *f'tas*, the large, specially woven blue and crimson kerchief. (See the photograph by the pioneering Greek photographer Nelly's [1899-1998] of women wearing the local costume of Skyros, fig. 16.)

Fig. 16. Women wearing the costumes of Skyros, Sporades, in the Panathenaic Stadium, Athens. Photo: Nelly's. Late 1930s.
Peloponnesian Folklore Foundation Photographic Archive, Nafplio

21

Chrysomándilo, bridal or festive costume

Astypalaia, Dodecanese. *c.* 1870

Peloponnesian Folklore Foundation, Nafplio

This bridal or festive costume of Astypalaia, the *chrysomándilo*, belonged to the Palatianos family and, according to Irini (Rinaki) Palatianou, it had been passed down through four generations starting with her great-grandmother, who was born around 1850. The *chrysomándilo* takes its name from the gold-embroidered, pearl-encrusted frontlet of its headdress. The basis of the headdress consists of the *margaritarénia skoúfia* (pearl-encrusted cap), the *kouloúra* (coil) and the two *bólies*, one yellow (called *asiménia*, literally 'silver') and the other white with embroidered ends (the *panomoustouchiá*). The headdress is secured with long silver pins (*kombovelónes*) and decorated with artificial flowers at the temples. The *skolopendráto* chemise is renowned for its embroideries, which cover the whole of the sleeves (fig. 17). The sleeved silk dress (*zatoúni*) is made of flowered satin imported from Constantinople. The ornaments include *vérges* (earrings), the *zonári* (sash) and the two *zosiés* forming the chain-link belt with its *kremasídi* (pendant). (For another form of the women's costume of Astypalaia, the *skléta*, which was the second-best festive costume, see cat. no. 22.)

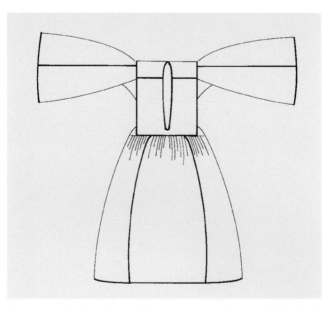

Fig. 17. Pattern of a chemise of the costume of Astypalaia, Dodecanese. Peloponnesian Folklore Foundation Archive, Nafplio

22

The dress of the *skléta* costume
Astypalaia, Dodecanese. Early 20th century
Peloponnesian Folklore Foundation, Nafplio
1977.06.0235

The dress is made of green satin and has shoulder straps and a gathered skirt with broad horizontal pleats. The lining is of off-white material. (For another form of the women's costume of Astypalaia, the *chrysomándilo*, which was the bridal or festive costume, see cat. no. 21.)

23

Women's costume
Psara, North-East Aegean Islands. Early 20th century
Peloponnesian Folklore Foundation, Nafplio

This costume was assembled by the Lyceum Club of Greek Women, Athens, out of two donations.

The women's costume of Psara belongs to a type that appears to have been worn in varying forms on other Aegean islands as well. It is renowned for its pure silk *tsiboukotó* chemise. The dark sleeveless dress has a richly pleated skirt with the characteristic horizontal pleat about 20 centimetres above the hem, which has a decorative strip of brocade. This horizontal pleat is found in nearly all island-type dresses. The headdress with its pure silk *bólia* is also very typical of island costumes. The Psara *bólia* combines well with the hairstyle, which anchors it to the forehead.

Towards the end of the 19th century, the painter Filippos Margaritis (1810-1892), who was also the first Greek professional photographer, took a photograph of a woman of Psara wearing the local costume (fig. 18).

Fig. 18. A woman of Psara,
North-East Aegean Islands.
Photo: Filippos Margaritis. Late 19th century.
Peloponnesian Folklore Foundation
Photographic Archive, Nafplio

24

Women's costume
Spetses, Saronic Islands. Early 20th century
Peloponnesian Folklore Foundation, Nafplio

The costumes of Spetses (for the pattern, see fig. 21), Hydra and the Ermionida region generally (for costumes of the Saronic Islands, see also fig. 36) used to have a pleated green dress with a crimson velvet hem and a *zipoúni* of European or Eastern brocade. Later, the dress of the Spetses costume was replaced by one made in the fashion of the day, while still retaining the everyday or festive headscarf (*piétes*), which might or might not be embroidered, or the *tsembéri*, which was carefully arranged on the head and held in place with special brooches, such as the *márka*, *kofináki* or *heráki*. Eventually the *zipoúni* – which was much the same as the *zipoúni* used in the 'Amalia' costume – was abandoned.

Laskarina Bouboulina (1711-1825), a native of Spetses and a legendary figure of the Greek War of Independence, was portrayed in a lithograph by Peter von Hess (1792-1871) – who also painted the monumental picture of King Otto's entry into Nafplio – dressed in the costume of Spetses during the blockade of Nafplio in the summer of 1821 (fig. 19). The painter Karl Krazeisen (1794-1878), a Philhellene who fought as a volunteer in the Greek War of Independence and painted portraits of the foremost personalities in the struggle for national liberation, painted a landscape of Aegina with women wearing the costume

Fig. 19. Peter von Hess,
Bobolina [Bouboulina]
Blockades Nauplia,
tinted lithograph, 28 x 21 cm.
From his album *Befreiung
Griechenlands in XXXIX Bildern
entworfen von Peter Hess*.
Benaki Museum, Athens

Fig. 20. Karl Krazeisen, *Aegina Landscape with Village Women at 'Kolona'*, 1827, watercolour, 26 x 31.5 cm.
National Gallery of Greece – Alexandros Soutzos Museum, Athens

of the Saronic Islands (fig. 20). The portraitist Francesco Pige (1822-1862), who made likenesses of members of well-known Greek seafaring families who were heavily involved and rose to prominence in the War of Independence, painted a portrait of Kyriakoula Kriezi, the daughter of Georgios Voulgaris (Governor of Hydra, 1802-1812), wearing the costume of her birthplace, Hydra; she is wearing a piece of jewellery bearing the royal insignia, which indicates her status as a member of Queen Amalia's personal entourage (fig. 22).

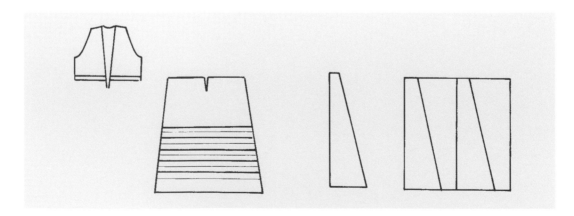

Fig. 21. Pattern of a dress of a costume of Spetses, Saronic Islands.
Peloponnesian Folklore Foundation Archive, Nafplio

Fig. 22. Francesco Pige, *Kyriakoula Voulgari, Wife of A. Kriezis*, c. 1850-1852, oil painting, 83 x 66 cm.
National Gallery of Greece – Alexandros Soutzos Museum, Athens,
E. Koutlidis Foundation Collection

25

Bridal or festive costume
Kastelorizo, Dodecanese. Late 19th century
Peloponnesian Folklore Foundation, Nafplio

The bridal or festive costume of Kastelorizo is also worn as the everyday form of dress. The *kondovrátsi* is a silk *vráka* gathered at the waist by the *vrakozóni* and tied round the leg below the knee. There it is decorated with a piece of gold brocade, the *káltsa tou vrakioú*. The chemise (locally called the *pekámiso*) is of white cotton-silk fabric and reaches only to the knees. The neck opening is done up with six round gold clasps, the *voúkles*; similar clasps are found in the Scandinavian countries. Over the chemise is the *kavádi* or *chrysós sákos*, a luxury dress open at the front below the neck. The *kavádi* is called by various names according to the material it is made of: *louloudáto*, *stroudáto*, *fidáto*, and so on. A sash (*zósma* or *tarapouloúz*) is wound several times round the waist: it is made up of three strips of material joined together lengthwise and comes from Tripoli in Lebanon.

The last garment to be put on is the *goúna*, a sort of outer garment made of gold-embroidered velvet and trimmed with fur all round. A small, round, soft red cap, the *raxíni*, is worn on the head, with the *tsakí* or *kaskí* round it like a crown: this is a band of stiff material swathed by a multicoloured silk kerchief, which often came from Tchilani (Kilani) in Cyprus. Pinned on to the *kaskí* is a brooch with one, two or three imitation gold coins, which anchors the *krépi*, a large silk shawl of Chinese (*kenéziko*) or Spanish (*spanióliko*) origin. The women of Kastelorizo wore a lot of jewellery, mainly rings on all their fingers, and used to walk with their arms crossed on their chests to display it.

26

Bridal or festive costume
Elymbos, Karpathos, Dodecanese. Early 20th century
Peloponnesian Folklore Foundation, Nafplio

The form of dress worn nowadays by the women of Elymbos is different from the old-style costume (see also fig. 23). In the old days, it was made of rich silk, gold-brocaded materials with embroideries and an abundance of jewellery. The whole costume is called the *kavá'i* (i.e. *kavádi*) after the principal garment. The costume shown here is a combination of the old and the new, as recorded by Tatiana Oikonomidou-Yiannara. It includes the *vráka*, a short bodice and a chemise, all made of white cotton or linen; the seams are sewn using the *repunta* stitch. Next comes the more recent *sakofoústano* or *sákos*, made up of a skirt and a *bólka*. The *sakofoústano*, under different names and made of different materials, was worn in all parts of Greece from the late 19th century. Over that are the *kavá'i*, made of striped silk, and the *chrysokóndosso*, a black felt jacket with gold embroidery all round. The sash round the *kavá'i* is made of printed black calico folded lengthwise four times and knotted in front. The footwear consists of knitted orange stockings and *yiminiá*, a sort of slipper with patent-leather uppers. In the headdress, the innermost items are two kerchiefs (the *antitsémbera*) forming the *gýros*. The *lahoúri*, or *mallítiko*, is a black outer kerchief of fine woollen material imported from Constantinople or Smyrna; its two ends are tied in a large knot on one side, just above the ear. Sewn on along both long sides are the *pitsília* (decorative beads). The ornaments attached to the headdress are the *gázi*, or *gándzi*, and the *koutelítis*; the earrings are called *skolarítsia*, or *kambánes*; round the neck are the *ambrákami* and the *myrimídia*; and on the breast the *yordalíki*, or *ordalíki*, with its *klóni*, with *herákia* suspended from them, and a chain with three *gólfia*.

Fig. 23. Photo of women, men and *kanakares* (firstborn girls) of Karpathos, Dodecanese, wearing local costumes. Early 20th century. Peloponnesian Folklore Foundation Photographic Archive, Nafplio

27

Bridal costume
Alexandria (Gidas), Imathia, Macedonia. Early 20th century
Peloponnesian Folklore Foundation, Nafplio

This bridal costume was worn in about 50 villages in the plain of Yannitsa, an area then called Roumlouki, where Gidas (now Alexandria) is the most important village (see also fig. 24). The chemise is made of white cotton. The *anderí*, a black quilted coat dress, is worn only by brides. The *sayás*, an open-fronted dress of dark blue cotton, is lined on the inside, right and left, with panels of gold-embroidered velvet (*podiés*, 'aprons'), which are visible when the sides are turned back. The *podiés* are never turned back when the wearer is in mourning. The belt, embroidered with silver spangles, is worn round the waist over the *sayás*. The *kondóssi* (sleeved waistcoat) and *foúta* (apron) complete the ensemble. An essential part of the bridal costume is the pair of sewn-on velvet sleeves (*broumánika*). The bridal headdress looks like a helmet and is called *katsoúli me tis foúndes*: the *katsoúli* is the hard, egg-shaped part of the headdress (see also fig. 25), held in place on the crown of the head by a lock of hair taken from married women, which was never taken off, even in bed. Wrapped round the *katsoúli* are the three kerchiefs of the headdress, one black and two white. One of the white kerchiefs hangs down the back of the neck and is called the *peristéra* (dove). A good bridal *katsoúli* also has a pair of tassels. The hair is cut in a fringe. The costume is finished with jewellery and flowers.

Fig. 24. A woman wearing the bridal costume of Gidas, Imathia, Macedonia, in the Panathenaic Stadium, Athens. Photo: Nelly's. Late 1930s. Peloponnesian Folklore Foundation Photographic Archive, Nafplio

Fig. 25. Photo of a married woman
wearing the costume of Gidas, Imathia,
Macedonia. Early 20th century.
Peloponnesian Folklore Foundation
Photographic Archive, Nafplio

28

Bridal or festive costume
Soufli, Thrace. Early 20th century
Peloponnesian Folklore Foundation, Nafplio

The bridal or festive costume of Soufli differs from those of other places in Thrace. Its distinctive feature is the kaftan, a sleeved, open-fronted dress made of striped silk from Syria. The bias-cut side panels jut out sharply to the right and left at the hips. The chemise is of natural-coloured local silk. The costume is completed with a *thymiatí* apron of exquisite workmanship. Round the waist is an articulated copper belt of the Thracian type, the *koróna*, an engagement present from the bridegroom-to-be. Characteristic features of the distinctive headdress are the *mag'líka* and the silver *paoúnia*.

29

Bridal or festive costume
Stefanoviki, Magnesia, Thessaly. Early 20th century
Peloponnesian Folklore Foundation, Nafplio

The bridal or festive costume of Stefanoviki was the customary dress of nearly all the villages of eastern Thessaly, with variations from place to place. It consists of a dark chemise, an *anderí* and the *kondándero* (a kind of quilted *anderí* made of *taraklí*). Round the waist is a gold-embroidered belt (*zonári*), fastened over the apron with either the bridal buckle or the less elaborate *thilykotária*. The material of the apron matches the sleeve lining of the *kondándero*. The sleeveless velvet outer garment is called the *katifés*. The head is covered with a round cap (*féssi*) encircled by an improvised frontlet adorned with gold coins. Brides from poor families would hire this frontlet, the *kafássi*, from the local landowner. The kerchief is made of silk in an aubergine colour. The jewellery worn with the costume comprises a double *kioustéki* (silver belt), a *souyás*, *parádes* (gold coins), a bracelet and a *haimalí* (amulet). (See also the illustration of a woman wearing the Stefanoviki costume in the early 20th century, fig. 26.)

Fig. 26. Postcard depicting a woman wearing the costume of Stefanoviki, Magnesia, Thessaly. Early 20th century. Stamped: 'Τύπος Ενδυμασίας Θεσσαλής, Εκδότης Στεφ. Στουρνάρας εν Βόλω αριθ. 16' (Type of costume of Thessaly, Publisher Stef. Stournaras in Volos no. 16). Peloponnesian Folklore Foundation Photographic Archive, Nafplio

30

Bridal *sayás*, cotton coat dress
Pylaia, Thessaloniki. Late 19th century
H. 1.05 m
Peloponnesian Folklore Foundation, Nafplio
1985.06.0102

The bridal dress is made of olive-green material with appliqué panels of red cloth decorated with multicoloured embroideries and tassels. The shoulders, chest and sleeves are trimmed with gold braid (see also cat. no. 31).

31

Orange bridal *sayás*, silk coat dress
Asvestohori, Thessaloniki. Late 19th century
H. 1.14 m
Peloponnesian Folklore Foundation, Nafplio
· 1985.06.0105

The dress has red cloth with embroidered designs on the chest and on the turn-ups of the sleeves. The lining is of white material.

The *sayádes* characteristic of most of the costumes of the Macedonian lowlands are nearly always made of a cotton fabric in balanced plain weave or in twill. They may be left white or dyed dark green, blue or black, and they often have a glossy finish (by being heavily starched and then ironed) by a professional dyer. They are embroidered on the inside of the front flaps of the skirt (*podiés* or *skoútes*) and the turn-ups of the sleeves, so that the embroidery will be visible when they are turned back, except in the costume of Pylaia (formerly Kapoudzida), where they are never turned back. A specialist tailor and embroiderer, the *terzis*, cuts, sews and embroiders the *sayás*.

32

Women's costumes
Sifnos, Cyclades. Late 18th century
Peloponnesian Folklore Foundation, Nafplio

The costumes of Sifnos shown in this exhibition consist of a petticoat (*misofóri* or *mesofoústano*), a white chemise of fine material, a *kanalotí* skirt and a sleeveless waistcoat (*tsipfí* or *dzipoúni*). The long coat (*doulamás*) made of European brocade is trimmed with fur all round. The headdress consists of a distinctive kind of cap (*pína*, so named after the *Pinna* genus of shellfish) covered with a silk kerchief (*pétsa*) and held in place by a silk ribbon (*zostíra*).

Only a few specimens of firmly dated costumes or parts of costumes from the Cycladic Islands are to be found in museums and collections in Greece and abroad. All date from the late 18th century or early 19th. The Lyceum Club of Greek Women in Athens has one costume of Sifnos, and the Peloponnesian Folklore Foundation has two. The Benaki Museum in Athens has one costume of the same period from Andros, and the National Historical Museum, also in Athens, has one from Ios. All have much the same combination of garments. This ensemble was probably worn in other places besides the Cyclades, on the evidence of pictorial records (see, for example, the costume of the Cypriot lady, fig. 27).

Valuable evidence concerning Cycladic costumes in the late 18th century can be gleaned from the accounts written by foreign travellers, such as the French diplomat M.-G.-F.-A. de Choiseul-Gouffier (1752-1817), who paid his first visit to Greece in 1776 (figs 28, 29). In addition, the dolls dressed in traditional local costumes, donated by Queen Olga in 1914 to the Lyceum Club of Greek Women, provide additional documentation for the costumes of the Cyclades and of Greece as a whole (see cat. nos 33, 35).

Fig. 27. A Cypriot lady, painted on the tall case of a wooden grandfather clock. Her costume is reminiscent of that of Sifnos, Cyclades.
Ethnological Museum (The House of Hadjigeorgakis Kornesios), Nicosia

Fig. 28. *Femmes de l'isle de Siphanto* (Women from Sifnos [Cyclades]), copper engraving, 29 x 36 cm.
Drawn by J.-B. Hilaire, engraved by A.-J. Duclos. From M.-G.-F.-A. de Choiseul-Gouffier,
Voyage pittoresque de la Grèce, Paris 1782.
Peloponnesian Folklore Foundation, Nafplio
Donated by Pauline Johnstone

Fig. 29. *Dames de l'isle de Tine* (Women from Tinos [Cyclades]), copper engraving, 29 x 37 cm.
Drawn by J.-B. Hilaire, engraved by J.-L. Delignon. From M.-G.-F.-A. de Choiseul-Gouffier,
Voyage pittoresque de la Grèce, Paris 1782.
Peloponnesian Folklore Foundation, Nafplio
Donated by Pauline Johnstone

33

Porcelain doll dressed in local costume
Kimolos, Cyclades. 1912-1913
Lyceum Club of Greek Women, Athens
Donated by Queen Olga
AM 14493

In 1914 Queen Olga donated to the Lyceum Club of Greek Women in Athens a set of porcelain dolls dressed in local costumes. She brought them from London in 1912-1913, with the intention of sending them in pairs (one female and one male) to the regions of the then Greek world to have the dolls dressed in local traditional costumes. Each doll wears an accurate copy of the costume it represents and so preserves in minute detail all of its numerous garments and accessories, the cut of the garments, and the whole range of their designs, colours and decorative motifs. (On Cycladic costumes, see cat. no. 32; for the other doll with a regional costume from the collection of the Lyceum Club of Greek Women, see cat. no. 35.)

34

Urban women's costume
Pyrgos, Ilia, Peloponnese. Mid – late 19th century
Peloponnesian Folklore Foundation, Nafplio

The urban costume of Pyrgos is unique and was taken as the model for the 'Amalia' costume (see cat. no. 43). It consists of a white silk-cotton chemise with gold braid on the sleeves, a *kavádi* of pink and white brocade and an old-style *zipoúni* of crimson velvet adorned with braid, gold-brocaded ribbons and a little gold embroidery round the edges and on the shoulders. (See also the urban costume of Patras, cat. no. 35.)

35

Porcelain doll dressed in local costume

Patras. 1912-1913
Lyceum Club of Greek Women, Athens
Donated by Queen Olga
AM 14515

(See also the urban costume of Pyrgos, cat. no. 34, and cat. no. 33 for the other doll dressed in a local costume from the collection of the Lyceum Club of Greek Women.)

36

Urban women's dress

Ioannina, Epiros. Mid-19th century
Peloponnesian Folklore Foundation, Nafplio

The urban women's costume of Ioannina has a waisted dress of gold-brocaded pink material, open over the chest, with a high, upright collar. It has long open sleeves, either with straight edges or edged in the *serái kapáki* manner, under which the sleeves of the silk chemise can be seen. The short-sleeved coat is made of crimson cotton velvet and trimmed with braid, gold ribbons and gold embroidery. The ensemble is completed by a long, off-white *bólia* over the head, with multicoloured silk embroidery, warp fringes and little silk tassels in the colours of the embroidery. (For another form of the Ioannina urban costume, see cat. no. 37.)

37

Urban women's costume
Ioannina, Epiros. Mid-19th century
Peloponnesian Folklore Foundation, Nafplio

This is one of the many types of the urban costume of Ioannina (see cat. no. 36), distinguished by the presence of the *pirpirí*, a kind of outer garment of the Ottoman period shaped like a *doulamás*, or dolman. It was worn throughout the Balkans, with local variations. It has a pure silk *vráka* and a chemise of off-white *bibizári*. The *anderí* (see also cat. nos 39, 40, 41) is made of white brocade with gold stripes and small green flowers. From the early 19th century onwards we find this brocade, with variations, being used as a lining material in some *férmeles*, as well as in the wedding dress of Aspasia King (see cat. no. 38). Over the *anderí* is the *pirpirí*, made of dark felt with gold embroidery and braid forming a scalloped edge all round. Silver jewellery set with agates is characteristically worn with this particular costume.

38

Wedding dress of Aspasia King
Athens. 1830
H. 1.33 m
Peloponnesian Folklore Foundation, Nafplio
Donated by Ioanna Papantoniou
1998.06.111

The wedding dress of Aspasia King consists of a dress and jacket of white silk brocade with gold stripes and small green flowers (on the brocade, see cat. no. 37). The sleeveless dress is gathered below the bust, with a wide opening above. Round the hem there is a bias-cut band of the same material, scalloped at the top and trimmed with a gold cord; above it is the familiar pleat found on the dresses of all Greek costumes of this period. The sleeves of the jacket are very long and call to mind the *anderí* (see also cat. nos 39, 40, 41). On the inside of the dress is a handwritten note: 'Written by me her daughter Mrs. Claudius B. Lasell. Wedding dress of the wife of the Revd. Jonas King of Athens Greece, Mrs. A. Aspasia King, a native of Smyrna – born about the year 1810'. The dress was purchased from Christie's.

Written by me her daughter
Mrs. Claudius B. Lasell.

Wedding
Mrs. A. Aspa

...s of the wife of the Rev.d Jonas King of Athens
King. a native of Smyrna - born about the...

39

Anderí, yellow taffeta coat dress
Turkey. Late 19th century
H. 1.67 m
Peloponnesian Folklore Foundation, Nafplio
Donated by Ioanna Papantoniou
1998.06.0102

The *anderí*, a sort of coat dress, is trimmed round the edges with frills and *bibíla* done with silk thread. It has an off-white lining. On the back is an inscription in Arabic script. (See cat. nos 40, 41, also the urban costume of Ioannina, cat. no. 37, and the wedding dress of Aspasia King, cat. no. 38.)

Among the many watercolours and drawings by the artist and architect Gerasimos Pitzamanos (1787-1825) is this characteristic painting of a woman in a yellow *anderí*, dated approximately towards the end of the 1810s (fig. 30).

Fig. 30. Gerasimos Pitzamanos,
Three Sisters: Costume with Anderí **(inscribed by the painter: 'Costume col Anderia / 3 Sorele'), 1818/1820, watercolour on paper 31.5 x 22 cm. It depicts a female figure in a yellow *anderí*. National Historical Museum, Athens**

40

Anderí, purple brocade coat dress
Syria (?). Late 19th century
H. 1.45 m
Peloponnesian Folklore Foundation, Nafplio
Donated by Paul Ginis
1991.06.0283

The purple material is brocaded with multicoloured plant designs. The *anderí* has a low, upright collar and long, slit sleeves, lined with a pale blue print. It is slit at the sides, nearly up to the waist, and scalloped all round, with an edging of gold cord. The lining is of white cotton. (See also cat. nos 39, 41, also the urban costume of Ioannina, cat. no. 37, and the wedding dress of Aspasia King, cat. no. 38.)

41

Anderí, red silk coat dress
Turkey. Late 19th century
H. 1.32 m
Peloponnesian Folklore Foundation, Nafplio
Donated by Ioanna Papantoniou
1999.06.0005

The silk fabric is embroidered with plant designs in gold thread. The *anderí* has an upright collar with an embroidered black velvet facing, and long slit sleeves lined with mauve and red satin. It is also slit down the sides. The garment is decorated with gold braid, priestly gold passementerie, gold cord and beige lace with blue floral designs all round. It is lined with earthy-coloured cotton with a floral print.

The *anderí* is a garment of Eastern origin (see also cat. nos 39, 40, the urban costume of Ioannina, cat. no. 37, and the wedding dress of Aspasia King, cat. no. 38.) It has very long sleeves, slit on the inner side, either with straight edges or edged in the *serái kapáki* manner. It is usually open down the front, sometimes with no fastenings and sometimes with a few home-made spherical buttons. It has an upright collar and always has long or short slits at the sides. All the edges are trimmed with braid, strips of lace or even gold embroidery. Many of the red *anderí* with all-over embroidery were later remade as *kondogoúnia* for the 'Amalia' costume (see cat. no. 42).

42

Kondogoúni, jacket made from a Turkish *anderí* for the 'Amalia' costume

Peloponnese (?). Mid-19th century
H. 0.34 m
Peloponnesian Folklore Foundation, Nafplio
Donated by Ioanna Papantoniou
1990.6.438

The *kondogoúni* is made of red cotton, embroidered all over with gold thread and spangles in plant designs. All the openings are edged with braid and the lining is purple. It was remade from a Turkish *anderí*. (See also cat. nos 39, 40, 41.)

43

'Amalia' costume
Athens. Late 19th century
Peloponnesian Folklore Foundation, Nafplio

The urban costume of the Peloponnese (see cat. no. 34) spread to other parts of Greece after 1837, when Amalia, the first Queen of Greece, adopted it as the official court dress, combining the Biedermeier style with the local *kavádi* and *zipoúni*. This costume was widely worn in Athens, among other places (fig. 31). The dress (*kavádi*) is made of taffeta, with an open bodice to show the neck opening of the chemise. The *kondogoúni* is of aubergine velvet, gold-embroidered and very close-fitting. The cap is a kalpak (*kalpáki*). Married women wore a tasselled flat round cap (*papaz'*), which they covered with black lace when they went to church.

Nikiphoros Lytras (1832-1904), one of the most important Greek painters and art teachers in the 19th century, also contributed to the development of bourgeois portraiture. Among others, he painted a monumental full-length portrait of Queen Amalia wearing the costume she herself had devised for her court (fig. 32).

Before the arrival of King Otto and Queen Amalia in Greece in 1837 and the establishment of the urban 'Amalia' costume, various different forms of dress were worn in Athens and its environs: an example can be seen in the lithograph by Louis Dupré (1789-1837) entitled *Mariage grec à Athènes* (Greek wedding in Athens), a product of his tour of Greece in 1819 (fig. 33).

Fig. 31. Gerasimos Pitzamanos,
Athenian Lady with her Young Daughter
(inscribed by the painter:
'Signora nobile della classe degli
arconti di Atene / Colla sua figlieta'), 1818,
watercolour on paper, 31.5 x 22 cm.
National Historical Museum, Athens

Fig. 32. Nikiphoros Lytras, *Amalia*, 1893,
oil painting, 260 x 150 cm.
Society for the Promotion of Education and Learning
[Philekpaideutiki Etaireia] Gallery, Athens

Fig. 33. Louis Dupré, *Mariage grec à Athènes* (Greek wedding in Athens),
hand-coloured lithograph, 38.5 x 32 cm.
From his book *Voyage à Athènes et à Constantinople,
ou collection de portraits, de vues et de costumes grecs et ottomans,
peints sur les lieux*, Paris 1825.
Alpha Bank Photographic Archive, Athens

44

'Amalia' costume with *satakroúta* skirt

Cyprus. Early 20th century

Peloponnesian Folklore Foundation, Nafplio

The newer costume with a skirt or full-length dress is of a Western type and came to Cyprus from liberated Greece as a variant of the 'Amalia' Greek national costume (fig. 32 and cat. no. 43), which was also worn by urban women all over the Balkans at the end of the 19th century. This ensemble has a pleated white cotton petticoat, a short chemise of off-white silk and a long gathered skirt made of local *satakroúta* (silk) with horizontal bands in an unusual combination of contrasting colours. Round the waist is a belt with a filigree buckle. The costume also includes a black felt jacket, the *sárka*, with gold ornamentation. The head is covered by a crimson print kerchief, the *kouroúkla me tin pipíla*. On feast days the kerchief was replaced by a soft cap (*féssi*) with one short black silk tassel attached radially to the crown and a second tassel hanging down to the shoulder on one side. The *féssi* was decorated with *pipíles* forming large flowers in relief.

45

Costume worn by the ladies-in-waiting of Queen Olga
Athens. Mid-19th century
Peloponnesian Folklore Foundation, Nafplio

The costume devised by Queen Olga for her ladies-in-waiting (fig. 34) was inspired by the bridal costume of the Mesogeia region of Attica. Perhaps its most distinctive innovation was the addition of a long train, a feature Queen Olga imported from Russia and prescribed for the ladies of the court. For its undergarment it has a long, pleated taffeta petticoat with its bodice stiffened with whalebone. Next come a short chemise of pure silk and a skirt of *bibizári*, with gold trimmings. The first skirt is covered by another one of felt with a long oval train, with a hook-and-eye fastening at the front; it is trimmed with a broad, pale blue velvet border. Over these is a short sleeveless coat reminiscent of the *gríza* of the bridal costume of Attica, decorated in the same way as the train. The pale blue borders were exclusively for the ladies-in-waiting; for members of the royal family, the queen opted for red. Athenian society ladies could choose whatever colour they liked except those two. To complete the ensemble there were a kalpak, a diadem, a buckle, long white kid gloves, a long *bólia* of *bimbizári* with gold lace along its length and a broad band of gold crochet lace and fringes at the ends. The shoes were always gold pumps. The costume was kept in a metal chest lined with wood to prevent the gold embroideries from becoming tarnished.

Fig. 34. Photo of Queen Olga wearing the costume
she established for her court, taken in 1868.
Peloponnesian Folklore Foundation Photographic Archive, Nafplio
Donated by Ioanna Papantoniou

46

Festive costume
Kifissia, Attica. Early 20th century
Peloponnesian Folklore Foundation, Nafplio

The festive costume of Kifissia consists of a sleeveless cotton chemise, the *foúndi*, with multicoloured embroidery on the hem, sometimes extending as far up as the knees. Clasping the upper torso is the *dzákos me ta katománika* (a tight-fitting bodice with sewn-on lower sleeves), and round the waist is a red belt. Next comes the *yoúrda*, the sleeveless coat with embroidery in dark wool. The hair is parted in the middle into two plaits, with silver ornaments (the *masoúr' plexídes*) hanging from them. Suspended from the shoulders are rows of chains with imitation coins.

Typical representations of the costumes of Attica in the first half of the 19th century can be seen in Otto Magnus von Stackelberg's engraving entitled *Paysanne des environs d'Athènes en habit de fête* (fig. 35; see also fig. 9) and in the painting by the French artist and Philhellene Pierre Bonirote (1811-1891) entitled *Danse grecque* (fig. 36; see also figs 19, 20, 21 and cat. no. 24).

Fig. 35. Otto Magnus von Stackelberg, *Paysanne des environs d'Athènes* (Village woman from the vicinity of Athens), hand-coloured copper engraving, 26 x 20 cm.
From his book *Costumes et usages des peuples de la Grèce moderne*, Rome 1825.
Alpha Bank Photographic Archive, Athens

Fig. 36. Pierre Bonirote, *Danse grecque* (Greek dance),
oil painting, 159.5 x 209 cm.
Archbishop Makarios III Foundation, Cultural Center, Nicosia

47

Bridal or festive costume
Corfu, Ionian Islands. Early 20th century
Peloponnesian Folklore Foundation, Nafplio

In the bridal or festive costume of Corfu (fig. 37), the undergarments are a white bodice and the *rokéto*, a gathered petticoat of fine calico. Over those is the skirt (*veléssi* or *ábito*) of pale blue taffeta with a gold-embroidered hem. The chest is covered by the white *boustína*, a knitted white dickey. The waist belt is called the *chrysózoni* or *chrysokímero*. Next comes the *zipoúni*, a short sleeveless waistcoat which leaves the whole of the bust exposed and is fastened with gold cufflinks (*fioúmbes*). The outer, sleeved *kondogoúni* (the *pesselí* or *krémezo*) is made of garnet-red velvet adorned with gold embroidery. The bridal apron is made of white tulle and covered all over with multicoloured wool embroidery and with bows and stars made of multicoloured ribbons. The headdress (*yiádema* or *stólos*) is worn by the bride for the first time on her wedding day, and from then on she wears it every day for the rest of her life. The old hairstyle has been replaced by the *torkós*, a sort of 'wreath' formed of four long black coils of hair (*boumbária*) bound with red ribbons (*staftádes*). It is adorned with flowers, little mirrors, fine wire spirals, feathers and the *bólia*, which is starched and attached to the back of the *torkós*, rising to a high peak in front. An essential accessory of the *torkós* is a peacock feather. The earrings are *vérges* and *kambánes*, and round the neck is a chain fastened to a filigree brooch on the chest called the *ílios*. Three more gold brooches of different sizes are known as the *spíles*. Another indispensable item is the *stavrós me tin koróna*, embellished with pearls and multicoloured semi-precious stones.

Fig. 37. Postcards depicting women wearing the costumes of Corfu, Ionian Islands. Early 20th century. Peloponnesian Folklore Foundation Photographic Archive, Nafplio

Sources – Bibliography

The Development of Costume in the Sphere of Influence of Greek Civilisation
Ioanna Papantoniou

BIBLIOGRAPHY

BOUCHER, FRANÇOIS (1967), *A History of Costume in the West*, London, Thames & Hudson.

BROUDY, ERIC (1979), *The Book of Looms: A History of the Handloom from Ancient Times to the Present*, Hanover/London, Brown University Press.

BURNHAM, DOROTHY K. (1973), *Cut my Cote*, Toronto, Royal Ontario Museum.

CAPIZZI, CARMELO, and GALATI, FRANCESCO (1989), *Piazza Armerina: The Mosaics and Morgantina*, Bologna, Italcards.

CAUBET, ANNIE (1998), *L'art des modeleurs d'argile. Antiquités de Chypre, Coroplastique*, vol. II, Paris, Musée du Louvre, no. 525.

EDEY, MAITLAND ARMSTRONG (1979), *Lost World of the Aegean*, New York, Time-Life Books.

ΙΣΤΟΡΙΑ ΤΟΥ ΕΛΛΗΝΙΚΟΥ ΕΘΝΟΥΣ [History of the Greek nation] (1971), vol. II, Athens, Ekdotike Athenon.

KARAMANOS, K. M. (n.d.), «Η ενδυμασία εν τω αρχαίω κόσμω» [Clothing in the ancient world], in *Μεγάλη Ελληνική Εγκυκλοπαίδεια Π. Δρανδάκη* [Great Greek encyclopaedia P. Drandakis], Athens, vol. XI: 146-148.

PAPANTONIOU, IOANNA (1996a), *Ελληνικές τοπικές ενδυμασίες* [Greek regional costumes], Nafplio, Peloponnesian Folklore Foundation.

— (1996b), «Η φορεσιά σε μια θεατρική παράσταση» [Costume in a theatrical production], in *Πρακτικά της Συνάντησης Στελεχών Χορευτικών Συγκροτημάτων* [Proceedings of the 1st workshop of dance company managers], Drama, Lyceum Club of Greek Women.

RUTSCHOWSCAYA, MARIE-HÉLÈNE (1990), *Coptic Fabrics*, Paris, Éditions Adam Biro.

SAKELLARAKIS, YANNIS, and SAPOUNA-SAKELLARAKI, EFI (1991), *Κρήτη Αρχάνες* [Crete: Archanes], Athens, Ekdotike Athenon.

STACKELBERG, OTTO MAGNUS VON (1825), *Costumes et usages des peuples de la Grèce moderne*, Rome.

VERNARDAKIS, ATHANASIOS N. (1906), *Περί αμφιέσεως* [On costume], Athens, offprint from *Imerisia* newspaper.

The Chemise of Greek Women's Local Costumes (19th – Early 20th Century)
Angeliki Roumelioti

BIBLIOGRAPHY

APOSTOLAKI, ANNA (1932), *Τα κοπτικά υφάσματα του εν Αθήναις Μουσείου Κοσμητικών Τεχνών* [Coptic fabrics in the Museum of Greek Folk Art], Athens, Archaeological Section of the Ministry of Education and Religion.

— (1952), «Βαφική. Βαφικαί ύλαι και χρήσις αυτών» [Dyeing: Dyestuffs and their use], *Laographia: Bulletin of the Greek Folklore Society* XIV: 72-124.

BOUCHER, FRANÇOIS (1967), *A History of Costume in the West*, London, Thames & Hudson.

BURNHAM, DOROTHY K. (1973), *Cut my Cote*, Toronto, Royal Ontario Museum.

DELITSIKOU-PAPACHRISTOU, MARIA (n.d.), *Η παραδοσιακή γυναικεία φορεσιά της Σκοπέλου* [The traditional women's costume of Skopelos], Skopelos, Municipality of Skopelos.

FRANGAKI, EVANGELIA (1974), *Η λαϊκή τέχνη της Κρήτης. Υφαντική και βαφική* [The folk art of Crete: Weaving and dyeing], vols I-II, Athens.

HATZIMICHALI, ANGELIKI (1925), *Ελληνική λαϊκή τέχνη. Σκύρος* [Greek folk art: Skyros], Athens.

— (1931), *Ελληνική λαϊκή τέχνη. Ρουμλούκι, Τρίκερι, Ικαρία* [Greek folk art: Roumlouki, Trikeri, Ikaria], Athens.

— (1948, 1954), *Ελληνικαί εθνικαί ενδυμασίαι* [Greek national costumes], illustrated by N. Sperling, vol. I: 1948, vol. II: 1954, Athens, Benaki Museum.

— (1956), «Τα χρυσοκλαβαρικά – συρματέινα – συρμακέσικα κεντήματα» [*Chrysoklavariká, syrmatéina* and *syrmakésika* embroideries], in *Mélanges offerts à Octave et Melpo Merlier à l'occasion du 25e anniversaire de leur arrivée en Grèce*, vol. 2, Athens, Institut Français d'Athènes: 447-449.

— (1963), «Οι φορεσιές της Αργολιδοκορινθίας» [The costumes of Argolidocorinthia], *Peloponnesiaki Protochronia* 7: 55-56.

— (1978, 1983), *Η ελληνική λαϊκή φορεσιά* [The Greek folk costume], vol. I (1978): *Οι φορεσιές με το σιγκούνι* [Costumes with the *sigoúni*], vol. II (1983): *Οι φορεσιές με το καβάδι* [Costumes with the *kavádi*], Athens, Benaki Museum and Melissa Publishing House.

HOUSTON, MARY G. (1934), *Ancient Greek, Roman and Byzantine Costume and Decoration*, London, Adam & Charles Black.

JOHNSTONE, PAULINE (1961), *Greek Island Embroidery*, London, A. Tiranti.

— (1972), *A Guide to Greek Island Embroidery*, London, Victoria and Albert Museum.

KAPETANAKI, SISSY, and PASSA-KOTSOU, MARIA (1983-1985), «Η έρευνα για τη νεοελληνική φορεσιά από τον 15ο ως τον 18ο αιώνα» [Research on Neohellenic costume from the 15th to the 18th century], *Ethnographika* 4-5, special issue, Nafplio, Peloponnesian Folklore Foundation: 45-50.

KARASTAMATI, ELENI (1975), «Εθνικές φορεσιές στο Βορειοελλαδικό χώρο» [National costumes in northern Greece], in *Πρακτικά Α' Συμποσίου Λαογραφίας του Βορειοελλαδικού Χώρου (Ήπειρος-Μακεδονία-Θράκη)* [Proceedings of the 1st symposium on the folklore of northern Greece (Epiros – Macedonia – Thrace)], Thessaloniki, 18-20 April 1974, Thessaloniki, Institute for Balkan Studies, no. 153: 125-131.

KOURIA, APHRODITE (1989), «Η παράσταση της ελληνικής φορεσιάς στα χαρακτικά των ευρωπαϊκών περιηγητικών εκδόσεων (15ος-19ος αι.)» [The depiction of Greek costume in prints in European travellers' books (15th-19th c.)], *Ethnographika* 7, Nafplio, Peloponnesian Folklore Foundation: 55-66.

KYRIAKIDOU-NESTOROS, ALKI (1983), *Τα υφαντά της Μακεδονίας και της Θράκης* [The textiles of Macedonia and Thrace], Athens, HOMMEH.

LAMBROU, ALIKI (1994), *Οι σκυριανές φορεσιές* [The costumes of Skyros], Nafplio, Peloponnesian Folklore Foundation.

LOUKOPOULOS, DIMITRIS (1927), *Πώς υφαίνουν και ντύνονται οι Αιτωλοί* [How the Aetolians weave and dress], Athens, I. N. Sideris Bookstore.

MAKRIS, KITSOS (1949), *Πηλιορείτικες φορεσιές* [Costumes of Pelion], Volos.

— (1976), *Η λαϊκή τέχνη του Πηλίου* [The folk art of Pelion], Athens, Melissa Publishing House.

MARINI, MARIA D. (1989), *Η μενιδιάτικη λαϊκή φορεσιά* [The folk costume of Menidi], Acharnes, Acharnes History and Folklore Society.

MICHAIL-DEDE, MARIA (1981), *Η φορεσιά της Μεσογείτισας* [The women's costume of the Mesogeia], Athens, Boyiatis Editions.

MINOTOU-LADA, MARIA, and GANGADI, DIANA (1993), *Ελληνικές φορεσιές. Συλλογή Εθνικού Ιστορικού Μουσείου* [Greek costumes: Collection of the National Historical Museum], Athens, Historical and Ethnological Society of Greece.

NAVARI, LEONORA (2006), *Η ελληνική ενδυμασία. Έντυπες πηγές 16ου-20ού αιώνα από τη Συλλογή Ι. Δ. Κοιλαλού* [Greek costume: Printed sources, 16th-20th centuries, from the I. D. Koilalous Collection], exhibition catalogue, Athens, Benaki Museum.

PAPANTONIOU, IOANNA (1974a), *Ελληνικές φορεσιές. Γυναικείες* [Greek costumes: Women's costumes], Nafplio, Peloponnesian Folklore Foundation.

— (1974b), «Φορεσιές της Μακεδονίας» [Costumes of Macedonia], *Makedoniki Zoi* 96, May: 24-31.

— (1975), «Φορεσιές της Θράκης» [Costumes of Thrace], *Makedoniki Zoi* 104, January: 26-31.

— (1976), «Οι χωρικές φορεσιές της Αργολιδοκορινθίας» [The village costumes of the Argolid and Corinthia], in *Πρακτικά Α' Διεθνούς Συνεδρίου Πελοποννησιακών Σπουδών* [Proceedings of the 1st international conference of Peloponnesian studies], vol. III, Sparta, 7-14 September 1975, Athens, Society for Peloponnesian Studies: 419-446.

— (1978), «Συμβολή στη μελέτη της γυναικείας ελληνικής παραδοσιακής φορεσιάς» [A contribution to the study of Greek women's traditional costumes], *Ethnographika* 1, Nafplio, Peloponnesian Folklore Foundation: 1-92.

— (1979), «Το βορειοελλαδικό πουκάμισο σε σχέση με τα πουκάμισα του υπόλοιπου ελληνικού χώρου» [The northern Greek chemise compared with the chemises of the rest of Greece], in *Πρακτικά Γ' Συμποσίου Λαογραφίας του Βορειοελλαδικού Χώρου (Ήπειρος-Μακεδονία-Θράκη)* [Proceedings of the 3rd symposium on the folklore of northern Greece (Epiros – Macedonia – Thrace)], Alexandroupoli, 14-18 October 1976, Thessaloniki, Institute for Balkan Studies, no. 186.

— (1981), *Ελληνικές φορεσιές* [Greek costumes], Nafplio, Peloponnesian Folklore Foundation.

— (1982), *Le costume régional grec*, Objets et mondes, Paris.

— (1983-1985), «Οι τοπικές φορεσιές στο Αιγαίο από την Άλωση μέχρι την Απελευθέρωση» [Local costumes in the Aegean from the fall of Constantinople to the liberation], *Ethnographika* 4-5, special issue, Nafplio, Peloponnesian Folklore Foundation: 29-44.

— (1985), *Η ελληνική γυναικεία φορεσιά και το κόσμημα άλλοτε και τώρα* [Greek women's costume and jewellery past and present], Athens, Ministry of Culture/Peloponnesian Folklore Foundation.

— (1991), *Ελληνικές φορεσιές. Συλλογή Λυκείου των Ελληνίδων Καλαμάτας* [Greek costumes: Collection of the Lyceum Club of Greek Women, Kalamata], Athens, Ekdotike Athenon.

— (1992), *Μακεδονικές φορεσιές* [Macedonian costumes], Nafplio, Peloponnesian Folklore Foundation.

— (2000), *Η ελληνική ενδυμασία. Από την αρχαιότητα ως τις αρχές, ιου 200ύ αιώνα* [Greek clothing: From antiquity to the early 20th century], Athens, Commercial Bank of Greece.

PAPANTONIOU, IOANNA, and PASSA-KOTSOU, MARIA (1988), *Λαογραφικό Μουσείο Ναυπλίου. Κατάλογος* [Nafplio Folklore Museum: Catalogue], Nafplio, Peloponnesian Folklore Foundation.

POLYCHRONIADI, ELENI (1980), *Ελληνικά κεντήματα* [Greek embroidery], Athens, Benaki Museum.

SAMPSON, ADAMANTIOS (1970), «Η λαϊκή φορεσιά της Σκοπέλου και Αλοννήσου» [The folk costume of Skopelos and Alonnisos], *Archeion Thessalikon Meleton* 5: 95-137.

TARSOULI, ATHINA (1941), *Ελληνικές φορεσιές* [Greek costumes], Athens, V. Papachrysanthou Lithographic Press.

— (1947), *Δωδεκάνησα* [The Dodecanese], vols I-III, Athens, I. M. Skazikis Alpha Editions.

THEOTOKI, ELISABETH-LULU (1994), *Ενδυμασίες Κερκύρας, Παξών και Διαποντίων Νήσων* [Costumes of Corfu, Paxi and the Diapontia Islands], Athens, Municipality of Corfu.

TSANGALAS, KONSTANTINOS (1982), *Η γυναικεία καραγκούνικη ενδυμασία σε μια θεσσαλική κοινότητα: κατασκευή και λειτουργία. Συμβολή στη μελέτη της ενδυμασίας στο φυσικό της περιβάλλον* [The women's costume of the Karagounides in a Thessalian community: Construction and function. A contribution to the study of dress in its natural environment], Ioannina.

— (1985), *Μια παλαιότερη μορφή της γυναικείας καραγκούνικης ενδυμασίας γύρω στα 1900. Λειτουργία, εξέλιξη, εγκατάλειψη* [An older form of the women's costume of the Karagounides, c. 1900: Function, evolution, abandonment], Ioannina.

— (1993), *Η γυναικεία καραγκούνικη ενδυμασία ιδιαίτερα σε μια θεσσαλική κοινότητα: κατασκευή και λειτουργία. Συμβολή στη μελέτη της ενδυμασίας στο φυσικό της περιβάλλον* [The women's costume of the Karagounides, particularly in a Thessalian community: Construction and function. A contribution to the study of dress in its natural environment], Athens, HOMMEH.

TSIGAKOU, FANI-MARIA (1980), *Η ελληνική ενδυμασία. Έντυπες πηγές 15ου-19ου αι.* [Greek costume: Printed sources, 15th-19th c.], catalogue, Athens, Hellenic Society of Bibliophiles.

VLACHOS, MANOLIS (1994), *Louis Dupré. Ταξίδι στην Αθήνα και την Κωνσταντινούπολη* [Louis Dupré: Journey to Athens and Constantinople], Athens, I. S. Latsis Group.

WEALE-BADIERITAKI, JEAN-ANN (1980), *Το γυναικείο παραδοσιακό πουκάμισο της ηπειρωτικής Ελλάδας* [The traditional women's costume of mainland Greece], doctoral dissertation, Athens.

WEIR, SHELAGH (1989), *Palestinian Costume*, London, British Museum Publications.

WELTERS, LINDA (1981-1982), 'Greek Women's Chemises in American Collections', *Ethnographika* 3, Nafplio, Peloponnesian Folklore Foundation: 23-40.

— (1982), 'Greek Women's Chemises', *Dress* 8: 10-21.

— (1988), *Women's Traditional Costume in Attica, Greece*, Nafplio, Peloponnesian Folklore Foundation.

— (1989), 'Women's Traditional Dress in the Provinces of Argolida and Corinthia, Part I: Stability and Change', *Ethnographika* 7, Nafplio, Peloponnesian Folklore Foundation: 17-30.

— (1998), 'Women's Traditional Dress in Argolidocorinthia: Local Variations', *Ethnographika* 11, Nafplio, Peloponnesian Folklore Foundation: 133-175.

— (ed.) (1999), *Folk Dress in Europe and Anatolia: Beliefs about Protection and Fertility*, Oxford/New York, Berg.

ZOGRAFOU-KORRE, KATERINA (1985), *Μεταβυζαντινή - νεοελληνική εκκλησιαστική χρυσοκεντητική* [Post-Byzantine and Modern Greek ecclesiastical gold embroidery], Athens.

ZORA, POPI (1981), *Κεντήματα και κοσμήματα της ελληνικής φορεσιάς* [Embroideries and jewellery of Greek costumes], 2nd edn, Athens, Museum of Greek Folk Art, 1st edn 1966.

The Women's Costume of Astypalaia
Maria Passa-Kotsou

SOURCES

Peloponnesian Folklore Foundation (PFF): Archive of oral interviews, interview with Irini Palatianou by Ioanna Papantoniou and Maria Passa-Kotsou, Nafplio, 1985 (herein referred to as PFF interview 1985).

Personal papers of Maria Passa-Kotsou: Manuscript notes from field research on Astypalaia and in Athens, 1996 (herein referred to as Passa-Kotsou 1996).

BIBLIOGRAPHY

FRENCH, ANN (2009), 'The Greek Embroidery Collecting of R. M. Dawkins and A. J. B. Wace', in Llewellyn-Smith, Michael, Kitromilides, Paschalis, and Calligas, Eleni (eds), *Scholars, Travels, Archives: Greek History and Culture through the British School at Athens*, London, British School at Athens: 77-90.

HATZIMICHALI, ANGELIKI (1954), *Ελληνικαί εθνικαί ενδυμασίαι* [Greek national costumes], illustrated by N. Sperling, vol. II, Athens, Benaki Museum (vol. I 1948).

— (1978), *Η ελληνική λαϊκή φορεσιά. Οι φορεσιές με το σιγκούνι* [The Greek folk costume: Costumes with the *sigoúni*], Athens, Benaki Museum and Melissa Publishing House.

MACHA-BIZOUMI, NADIA [2003], «Το φωτογραφικό αρχείου του Αιμίλιου Λέστερ» [The photographic archive of Émile Lester], in *Ημερολόγιο 2004* [2004 diary], Athens, Lyceum Club of Greek Women.

MINOTOU-LADA, MARIA, and GANGADI, DIANA (2005), *Ελληνικές φορεσιές. Συλλογή Εθνικού Ιστορικού Μουσείου* [Greek costumes: Collection of the National Historical Museum], 2nd (expanded) edn, Athens, Historical and Ethnological Society of Greece (1st edn 1993).

MONTESANTO, MARICA (1930?), *L'Isola dei Gigli (Stampalia)*, preface Giuseppe Gerola, Rome, Sindacato Italiano Arti Grafiche (Collezione di Opere e di Monografie a Cura del Ministero delle Colonie No. 7).

PAPAMANOLI, LOULA (1986), *Το παραδοσιακό κόσμημα στα Δωδεκάνησα* [Traditional jewellery in the Dodecanese], [Athens], HOMMEH.

PAPANTONIOU, IOANNA (1978), «Συμβολή στην μελέτη της γυναικείας ελληνικής φορεσιάς» [A contribution to the study of Greek women's costumes], *Ethnographika* 1, Nafplio, Peloponnesian Folklore Foundation: 1-92.

— (1983-1985), «Οι τοπικές φορεσιές στο Αιγαίο από την Άλωση μέχρι την Απελευθέρωση» [Local costumes in the Aegean from the fall of Constantinople to the Liberation], *Ethnographika* 4-5, special issue, Nafplio, Peloponnesian Folklore Foundation: 29-44.

— (1991), *Ελληνικές φορεσιές. Συλλογή Λυκείου των Ελληνίδων Καλαμάτας* [Greek costumes: Collection of the Lyceum Club of Greek Women, Kalamata], Athens, Ekdotike Athenon.

— (1996), *Ελληνικές τοπικές ενδυμασίες* [Greek regional costumes], Nafplio, Peloponnesian Folklore Foundation.

PAPANTONIOU, IOANNA, POLITOU, XENIA, and ZIDIANAKIS, VASSILIS [1994], *Ημερολόγιο 1995. Τα μαντίλια και οι μπόλιες στις ελληνικές τοπικές φορεσιές* [1995 diary: Kerchiefs and headscarves in Greek local costumes], Athens, Peloponnesian Folklore Foundation.

PASSA-KOTSOU, MARIA [1988], «Εισαγωγή» [Introduction], in *Ημερολόγιο 1989* [1989 diary] (photographs by Émile Lester), Athens, Lyceum Club of Greek Women.

PATELLIS, YANNIS (2001), «Η Αστυπάλαια στο Αρχιπέλαγος της πειρατείας» [Astypalaia in the archipelago of piracy], *Kalymniaka Chronika* XIV, 'The Muses' Literary Society of Kalymnos: 79-88.

TARSOULI, ATHINA (1996), *Αστυπάλαια* [Astypalaia], anastatic reprint of *Δωδεκάνησα* [The Dodecanese] (vol. II), Athens, Society of Friends of Astypalaia (1st edn 1948).

WACE, ALAN J. B., and LAURENCE, WILLIAM (1914), *Catalogue of a Collection of Old Embroideries of the Greek Islands and Turkey*, exhibition catalogue, London, Burlington Fine Arts Club.

ZAIRI, MARIA (2001), «Η παραδοσιακή γυναικεία φορεσιά της Αστυπάλαιας» [The traditional women's costume of Astypalaia], *Kalymniaka Chronika* XIV, 'The Muses' Literary Society of Kalymnos: 53-78.

ZORA, POPI (1969), «Χρωματιστά κεντήματα» [Coloured embroideries], in Papadopoulos, Stelios (ed.), *Νεοελληνική χειροτεχνία* [Modern Greek handicrafts], Athens, National Bank of Greece: 162-189.

The 'Amalia' Costume: The Visual Symbol of the Transition from the Oriental Past to Western Modernity (19th Century)
Nadia Macha-Bizoumi

BIBLIOGRAPHY
ANTONIJEVIĆ, DRAGOSLAV (1983), 'Common Elements in the Town Costume Worn in Serbia and Greece in the 19th Century', *Balkan Studies* 24: 343-353.

BADA, KONSTANTINA (1983), *Η αθηναϊκή γυναικεία φορεσιά κατά την περίοδο 1687-1834. Ενδυματολογική μελέτη* [Athenian women's dress in the period 1687-1834: A study of clothing], doctoral dissertation, Ioannina, University of Ioannina.

— (1995), «Η παράδοση στη διαδικασία της ιστορικής διαπραγμάτευσης της εθνικής και τοπικής ταυτότητας. Η περίπτωση της φουστανέλας» [Tradition in the process of the historical negotiation of national and local identity], *Ethnologia* 4: 127-150.

BOUSE, VANA (2007), «Όθων και Αμαλία. Δύο φιλέλληνες στον ελληνικό θρόνο» [Otto and Amalia: Two philhellenes on the Greek throne], in *Η βασίλισσα Αμαλία, 1818-1875* [Queen Amalia, 1818-1875], tr. Stelios Lydakis, Athens, Museum of the City of Athens – Vouros-Eutaxias Foundation: 33-62.

DROULIA, LOUKIA (1999), «Οι ενδυματολογικές μεταλλαγές στα χρόνια της εθνικής διαμόρφωσης του νέου ελληνισμού» [Changing modes of dress in the years of the national formation of modern Hellenism], in *Πρακτικά Επιστημονικού Συμποσίου. Ο Ρομαντισμός στην Ελλάδα (12 και 13 Νοεμβρίου 1999)* [Proceedings of the symposium: Romanticism in Greece (12 and 13 November 1999)], Society for the Study of Modern Greek Culture and General Education: 127-145.

GATOPOULOS, DIMITRIS (1942), *Η ιστορία της αθηναϊκής κοινωνίας* [The history of Athenian society], Athens, Aetos Editions.

GELLNER, ERNEST (1992), *Έθνη και εθνικισμός* [Nations and nationalism], tr. Dora Lafazani, Athens, Alexandria Editions.

HASE-SCHMUNDT, ULRIKE VON (2007), «Μια προσωπογραφία της Αμαλίας, βασίλισσας της Ελλάδος, με εθνική ενδυμασία (1849)» [A portrait of Amalia, Queen of Greece, in national costume (1849)], in *Η βασίλισσα Αμαλία, 1818-1875* [Queen Amalia, 1818-1875], tr. Stelios Lydakis, Athens, Museum of the City of Athens – Vouros-Eutaxias Foundation: 257-268.

HOBSBAWM, ERIC (2010), 'Introduction', in Hobsbawm, Eric, and Ranger, Terence (eds), *The Invention of Tradition*, Cambridge University Press: 1-14.

KARPOZILOU, MARTHA (1991), *Ελληνικά οικογενειακά φιλολογικά περιοδικά, 1847-1900* [Greek family literary magazines, 1847-1900], Ioannina, University of Ioannina, Yearbook of the Primary Teacher Training Department, Appendix 1.

KASIMATI, MARILENA Z. (ed.) (2000), *Αθήνα-Μόναχο. Τέχνη και πολιτισμός στην νέα Ελλάδα* [Athens–Munich: Art and culture in modern Greece], exhibition catalogue, Athens, National Gallery of Greece – Alexandros Soutzos Museum, National Historical Museum.

KITROMILIDES, PASCHALIS (2000), «Δύο "νεοκλασσικά" βασίλεια στην εποχή του εθνικισμού» [Two 'Neoclassical' kingdoms in the age of nationalism], in Kasimati, Marilena Z. (ed.), *Αθήνα-Μόναχο. Τέχνη και πολιτισμός στην νέα Ελλάδα* [Athens–Munich: Art and culture in modern Greece], exhibition catalogue, Athens, National Gallery of Greece – Alexandros Soutzos Museum, National Historical Museum: 33-37.

LURIE, ALISON (1983), *The Language of Clothes*, New York: Vintage Books.

MACHA-BIZOUMI, NADIA (2012), 'Amalia Dress: The Invention of a New Costume Tradition in the Service of Greek National Identity', *Catwalk: The Journal of Fashion, Beauty and Style* 1/1: 65-90.

PAPANTONIOU, IOANNA (2000), *Η ελληνική ενδυμασία. Από την αρχαιότητα ως τις αρχές του 20ού αιώνα* [Greek clothing: From antiquity to the early 20th century], Athens, Commercial Bank of Greece.

RUBINSTEIN, RUTH (1995), *Dress Codes: Meanings and Messages in American Culture*, San Francisco/Oxford, Westview Press.

SKAFIDAS, MICHAEL (2009), 'Fabricating Greekness: From Fustanella to the Glossy Page', in Paulicelli, Eugenia, and Clark, Hazel (eds), *The Fabric of Cultures: Fashion, Identity, and Globalization*, London/New York, Routledge: 145-163.

SKOPETEA, ELLI (1988), *Το «Πρότυπο Βασίλειο» και η Μεγάλη Ιδέα. Όψεις του εθνικού προβλήματος στη Ελλάδα (1830-1880)* [The 'Model Kingdom' and the Great Idea: Aspects of the national problem in Greece (1830-1880)], Athens, Polytypo Editions.

VERINIS, JAMES (2005), 'Spiridon Loues, the Modern *Foustanela*, and the Symbolic Power of *Pallikaria* at the 1896 Olympic Games', *Journal of Modern Greek Studies* 23: 139-175.

VITKOVIĆ-ŽIKIĆ, MILENA (2009), 'Ptychoseis in Serbian City-wear', *Endymatologica* 3, *Πρακτικά Συνεδρίου «Η μελέτη των πτυχώσεων: πολλαπλές ερμηνείες»* [Proceedings of the conference on 'Folds and pleats: Multiple meanings'] (Athens, 21-25 June 2004), Nafplio, Peloponnesian Folklore Foundation: 118-123.

The Costume of the Ladies-in-Waiting to Queen Olga: Court Elegance Using Local Materials
Xenia Politou

BIBLIOGRAPHY
ALYOSHINA, T. S., *et al.* (1977), *History of Russian Costume from the Eleventh to the Twentieth Century*, exhibition catalogue, New York, Metropolitan Museum of Art.

BOZI, SOULA (1991), *Τα μεταξωτά της Προύσας. Από το κουκούλι στο μετάξι και τα μεταξωτά υφάσματα* [The silks of Brusa: From the cocoon to silk and silk fabrics], Athens.

FOTOPOULOS, DIONYSSIS (1999), *Το ένδυμα στην Αθήνα στο γύρισμα του 19ου αιώνα* [Athenian fashions at the turn of the 19th century], Athens, ELIA (Hellenic Literary and Historical Archive).

HATZIMICHALI, ANGELIKI (1948, 1954), *Ελληνικαί εθνικαί ενδυμασίαι* [Greek national costumes], illustrated by N. Sperling, vol. I: 1948, vol. II, 1954, Athens, Benaki Museum.

— (1978), *Η ελληνική λαϊκή φορεσιά. Οι φορεσιές με το σιγκούνι* [The Greek folk costume: Costumes with the *sigoúni*], Athens, Benaki Museum and Melissa Publishing House.

KAROLOU, IOULIA (1934), *Όλγα η βασίλισσα των Ελλήνων (22 Αυγούστου 1851 – 19 Αυγούστου 1926)* [Olga, Queen of the Greeks (22 August 1851 – 19 August 1926)], Athens, Hestia.

KOSTI, CHRISTINA N. (1948-1949), *Αναμνήσεις εκ της αυλής Γεωργίου Α΄* [Reminiscences from the court of George I], Athens.

MINOTOU-LADA, MARIA, and GANGADI, DIANA (2005), *Ελληνικές φορεσιές. Συλλογή Εθνικού Ιστορικού Μουσείου* [Greek costumes: Collection of the National Historical Museum], 2nd (expanded) edn, Athens, Historical and Ethnological Society of Greece (1st edn 1993).

MACHA-BIZOUMI, NADIA (2012), 'Amalia Dress: The Invention of a New Costume Tradition in the Service of Greek National Identity', *Catwalk: The Journal of Fashion, Beauty and Style* 1/1: 65-90.

MARINI, MARIA D. (1989), *Η μενιδιάτικη λαϊκή φορεσιά* [The folk costume of Menidi], Acharnes, Acharnes History and Folklore Society.

MICHAIL-DEDE, MARIA (1981), *Η φορεσιά της Μεσογείτισας* [The women's costume of the Mesogeia], Athens, Boyiatis Editions.

PAPADIMITRIOU, ELENI (1995), *Η μεταξουργία στην Κύπρο. Με αναφορά στην Λάπηθο και τον Καραβά* [The silk tradition in Cyprus: With reference to Lapithos and Karavas], Nicosia, Laiki Bank Cultural Centre.

PAPANTONIOU, IOANNA (1998), *Η γυναικεία φορεσιά της Αττικής* [The women's costume of Attica], Athens, Lyceum Club of Greek Women.

— (1999), «...και βάλαμε τα φράγκικα» ['...and we started wearing Western-style clothes'], in Fotopoulos, Dionyssis, *Το ένδυμα στην Αθήνα στο γύρισμα του 19ου αιώνα* [Clothes in Athens at the turn of the 19th century], Athens, ELIA (Hellenic Literary and Historical Archive): 47-53.

— (2000), *Η ελληνική ενδυμασία. Από την αρχαιότητα ως τις αρχές του 20ού αιώνα* [Greek clothing: From antiquity to the early 20th century], Athens, Commercial Bank of Greece.

— (2006), «Εισαγωγή» [Introduction], in *Χρυσοκέντητα. Η μαστοριά των τερζήδων* [Gold embroideries: The masterly skills of the *terzídes*], Kalamata, Kalamata Lyceum Club of Greek Women: n.p.

PAPANTONIOU, IOANNA, and KANELLOPOULOS, KANELLOS (1999), *25 χρόνια Πελοποννησιακό Λαογραφικό Ίδρυμα* [25 years, Peloponnesian Folklore Foundation], Nafplio, Peloponnesian Folklore Foundation.

PAPANTONIOU, IOANNA, and POLITOU, XENIA (eds) (2000), *Οι κούκλες της Βασίλισσας Όλγας* [The dolls of Queen Olga], Athens, Lyceum Club of Greek Women.

POLITOU, XENIA (2013), 'Transparence et dentelle dans le costume de cour de la reine Olga (1867-1913). Deux éléments empruntés aux costumes régionaux grecs', in *Dentelle, mode et transparence / Lace, Fashion and Transparency. ICOM's Costume Committee. Proceedings from the Annual Conference 21-27 October 2012 Bruxelles. Musée du Costume et de la Dentelle*, Brussels: 100-105.

SALTARIS, NIKOS (1986), *Η ζωή των Αρβανιτών* [The life of the Arvanites], Athens, Yeros Editions (Arvanitiki Vivliografia 1).

SPANTIDAKIS, YOULIE (2001), 'Le trousseau de S.A. la princesse Marie Bonaparte. Reportages de l'époque', *Endymatologica* 2, *Πρακτικά της 53ης Συνάντησης του Ενδυματολογικού Τμήματος του ICOM* [Proceedings of the 53rd meeting of the ICOM Costume Committee], Nafplio, Peloponnesian Folklore Foundation: 40-46.

WELTERS, LINDA (1988), *Women's Traditional Costume in Attica, Greece*, Nafplio, Peloponnesian Folklore Foundation.

ZORA, POPI (1994), *Ελληνική τέχνη. Λαϊκή τέχνη* [Greek art: Folk art], Athens, Ekdotike Athenon.

WEB PAGE

NICHOLSON, NICK (2013), 'Putting on the Armor: Women's Court Costume and Positions in Imperial Russia', *Alexander Palace Time Machine* (http://www.alexanderpalace.org/palace/ctCostume.html).

Revisiting Greek Elegance: Greek Local Costume as a Source of Inspiration for Contemporary Fashion and Costume Design
Sofia Pantouvaki

BIBLIOGRAPHY

BEYOND DRESS CODES: FROM TRADITIONAL COSTUME TO CONTEMPORARY FASHION, Nicosia, Laiki Bank Cultural Centre, Hellenic American Union and the Cyprus Fashion Designers Association.

FALIDA, EFI (2009), «Ελληνίδες θεές στο δρόμο» [Greek goddesses in the street], *Ta Nea* newspaper, 16 June, 4/22.

GALATIS, YANNIS (1985), *Για μια μόδα ελληνική* [Towards a Greek fashion], Athens, HOMMEH.

GEORGITSOYANNI, EVANGELIA N., and PANTOUVAKI, SOFIA (2011), 'Culture and Fashion: Greek Designer Yannis Tseklenis, a Case Study', in de Witt-Paul, Alissa, and Crouch, Mira (eds), *Fashion Forward*, Oxford: Inter-Disciplinary Press: 153-164.

KAMITSIS, LYDIA (2012), «Ερευνώντας τις παραδόσεις. Μια δημιουργική διαδικασία» [Studying traditions: A creative process], in *Beyond Dress Codes: From Traditional Costume to Contemporary Fashion*, Nicosia, Laiki Bank Cultural Centre, Hellenic American Union and the Cyprus Fashion Designers Association: 22-23.

LYBEROPOULOS, DIMITRIS (1999), *Ελληνική μόδα, 1900-2000. Ένας αιώνας δημιουργίας* [Greek fashion, 1900-2000: A century of creative activity], Athens: Artistic Events.

MACHA-BIZOUMI, NADIA (2010), «"Ο βοσκός, η Σαρακατσάνα και η κάπα του βοσκού στην ελληνική μόδα". Η ελληνική τοπική φορεσιά στην πασαρέλα της μόδας (1960-1970). Το παράδειγμα του Λυκείου των Ελληνίδων» ['The shepherd, the Sarakatsan woman and the shepherd's cape in Greek fashion': Greek local costume on the catwalk (1960-1970). The example of the Lyceum Club of Greek Women], in Papantoniou, Ioanna (ed.), *Ενδύεσθαι. Προς ένα Μουσείο Πολιτισμού του ενδύματος* [Endyesthai (to dress): Towards a costume culture museum], exhibition catalogue, Nafplio, Peloponnesian Folklore Foundation: 99-107.

PANTOUVAKI, SOFIA (2009), 'Pleats as an Element of Form and Decoration in the Work of Greek Scenographer Laloula Chryssikopoulou', in *Endymatologika 3*, *Πρακτικά Συνεδρίου «Η μελέτη των πτυχώσεων: πολλαπλές ερμηνείες»* (Αθήνα, 21-25 Ιουνίου 2004) [Proceedings of the conference on 'Folds and pleats: Multiple meanings' (Athens, 21-25 June 2004)], Nafplio, Peloponnesian Folklore Foundation: 22-28.

— (2013), «Ο λαϊκός πολιτισμός ως εκφραστικό μέσο στη σύγχρονη ελληνική σκηνογραφία-ενδυματολογία (1985-2010)» [Popular culture as an expressive medium in contemporary Greek stage and costume design (1985-2010)], in *Πρακτικά του Συνεδρίου 'Λαϊκός πολιτισμός και έντεχνος λόγος (Ποίηση – Πεζογραφία – Θέατρο)'* [Proceedings of the conference on 'Popular culture and literature (poetry – prose – drama)'] (Athens, 8-12 December 2010), Athens, Hellenic Folklore Research Centre of the Academy of Athens: 243-254 and Appendix 6-12.

PAPANTONIOU, IOANNA (2010), «Ενδύεσθαι – Προσεγγίσεις. Το σκεπτικό μιας έκθεσης» [Endyesthai – approaches: The rationale underlying an exhibition], in Papantoniou, Ioanna (ed.), *Ενδύεσθαι. Προς ένα Μουσείο Πολιτισμού του ενδύματος* [Endyesthai (to dress): Towards a costume culture museum], Nafplio, Peloponnesian Folklore Foundation: 15-27.

PELOPONNESIAN FOLKLORE FOUNDATION [PFF] (2006), *6 Παγκόσμιοι Έλληνες σχεδιαστές μόδας* [6 Greek fashion designers of worldwide renown], exhibition catalogue, Nafplio.

POLITOU, XENIA (2010), «Από τον σχεδιαστή στην πελάτισσα, και από την γκαρνταρόμπα στο μουσείο. Μια πρόταση συλλεκτικής πολιτικής για ένα μουσείο πολιτισμού του ενδύματος» [From designer to customer and from wardrobe to museum: A proposed collection policy for a costume culture museum], in Papantoniou, Ioanna (ed.), *Ενδύεσθαι. Προς ένα μουσείο πολιτισμού του ενδύματος* [Endyesthai (to dress): Towards a costume culture museum], exhibition catalogue, Nafplio, Peloponnesian Folklore Foundation: 3-11.

TSEKLENIS, YANNIS (2000), «Ελληνική "βιομηχανία" μόδας» [A Greek fashion 'industry'], *Endymatologika 1*, Nafplio, Peloponnesian Folklore Foundation: 11-16.

—(2002), «Ελληνική και διεθνής μόδα στη σύγχρονη εποχή: Μια συνέντευξη του Γιάννη Τσεκλένη ο τον Ιωάννη Πετρόπουλο» [Greek and international fashion in the present day: Ioannis Petropoulos interviews Yannis Tseklenis], *Technes kai Archaiologia*, 84, September 2002: 52-63.

VRYONIDOU-YIANGOU, MARINA (2012), «Η εξέλιξη της παράδοσης. Η Κυπριακή λαϊκή τέχνη στη σύγχρονη μόδα» [The evolution of tradition: Cypriot folk art in contemporary fashion], in *Beyond Dress Codes: From Traditional Costume to Contemporary Fashion*, Nicosia, Laiki Bank Cultural Centre, Hellenic American Union and the Cyprus Fashion Designers Association: 19-20.

WEB PAGES

FALIDA, EFI (2010), «Η Καραγκούνα είναι και πάλι σικ» [The Karagouna is back in fashion], *Ta Nea* newspaper, 24 September (also online at www.archaiologia.gr/blog/2010/09/24/η-καραγκούνα-είναι-και-πάλι-σικ-2/).

GOMOUZA, IOANNA (2010), «Όταν η φουστανέλα εμπνέει!» [When the foustanella brings inspiration!], *Athinorama* magazine, 23 September (http://www.athinorama.gr/daylife/articles/?id=9491).

HELLENIC AMERICAN UNION (2010). *Beyond Dress Codes: Contemporary Fashion Designers in Dialogue with Traditional Greek Costume* (http://www.hau.gr/?i=culture.en.past_event&itemCode=beyonddress).

JONES, DOLLY (2009), 'John Galliano, Autumn/Winter 2009-10 Ready-to-wear', *Vogue Fashion Shows*, 11 March (www.vogue.co.uk/fashion/autumn-winter-2009/ready-to-wear/john-galliano).

KONSTANTINAKOU, PANAYIOTA (2013), 'From "Made in Greece" to "Made in China": A 21st Century Touring Revival of *Golfo*, a 19th-century Greek Melodrama', *Filmicon: Journal of Greek Film Studies*, No. 1, September (http://filmiconjournal.com/journal/article/2013/1/6).

KUSTENI, MATOULA (2010), «Τσολιά μου...» [My dear Evzone...], *Eleftherotypia* newspaper, *Epta* section, 19 September (http://www.enet.gr/?i=news.el.article&id=203760).

MORTON, CAMILLA (2006), 'Jean Paul Gaultier, Spring/Summer 2006 Couture', *Vogue Fashion Shows*, 26 January (www.vogue.co.uk/fashion/spring-summer-2006/couture/jean-paul-gaultier).

PISSALIDIS, YORGOS (2010), «Beyond Dress Codes. Όταν η Χατζημιχάλη συνάντησε τον Γκοτιέ» [Beyond dress codes: When Hatzimichali met Gaultier], *Ellinikes Grammes*, 4 October (http://www.e-grammes.gr/article.php?id=4517).

TAKIS (ongoing), *Forgotten Peacock*, www.forgottenpeacock.com.

Women's Fashion in England: The Influence of Ancient Greek Dress on the Dress Reform Movement of the Late 19th Century
Myrsini Pichou

SELECT BIBLIOGRAPHY
BURMAN BAINES, BARBARA (1981), *Fashion Revivals: From the Elizabethan Age to the Present Day*, London, B. T. Batsford.
CALLOWAY, STEPHEN, and FEDERLE ORR, LYNN (eds) (2011), *The Cult of Beauty: The Aesthetic Movement, 1860-1900*, exhibition catalogue, London, V&A Publishing.

CHALLIS, DEBBIE (2012), 'Fashioning Archaeology into Art: Greek Sculpture, Dress Reform and Health in the 1880s', *Journal of Literature and Science* 5/1: 53-69.

CUNNINGHAM, PATRICIA (2002), *Reforming Women's Fashion, 1850-1920: Politics, Health and Art*, Kent, OH, Kent State University Press.

EVANGELISTA, STEFANO (2009), *British Aestheticism and Ancient Greece: Hellenism, Reception, Gods in Exile*, Basingstoke/ New York, Palgrave Macmillan.

HAWEIS, Mrs H. R. (1883), *The Art of Beauty*, London, Chatto & Windus, 2nd edn.

JENKYNS, RICHARD (1980), *The Victorians and Ancient Greece*, Oxford, Basil Blackwell.

KAMITSIS, LYDIA (2004), «Περί του νεοκλασικισμού στη μόδα ή η ψευδαίσθηση της αρχαιότητας» [Neoclassicism in fashion and the illusion of antiquity], in Papantoniou, Ioanna (ed.), *Πτυχώσεις. Από το αρχαίο ελληνικό ένδυμα στη μόδα του 21ου αιώνα* [Ptychoseis = folds and pleats: Drapery from ancient Greek dress to 21st century fashion], exhibition catalogue, Athens, Peloponnesian Folklore Foundation / Hellenic Culture Organisation: 78-95.

KODA, HAROLD (2003), *Goddess: The Classical Mode*, exhibition catalogue, New Haven/London, The Metropolitan Museum of Art/Yale University Press.

LEE, VERNON (1884), *Miss Brown: A Novel*, vol. I, Edinburgh/London, William Blackwood & Sons.

NEWTON, STELLA MARY (1974), *Health, Art and Reason: Dress Reformers of the 19th Century*, London, John Murray.

OLIPHANT, Mrs (MARGARET) (1878), *Dress*, London, Macmillan & Co.

ORMOND, LEONÉE (1968), 'Female Costume in Aesthetic Movement of the 1870 and 1880s', *Costume: The Journal of the Costume Society* 2: 33-38.

OSMA, GUILLERMO DE (1980), *Mariano Fortuny: His Life and Work*, New York, Rizzoli.

PAPANTONIOU, IOANNA (1996), *Ελληνικές τοπικές ενδυμασίες* [Greek regional costumes], Nafplio, Peloponnesian Folklore Foundation.

— (2000), *Η ελληνική ενδυμασία. Από την αρχαιότητα ως τις αρχές του 20ού αιώνα* [Greek clothing: From antiquity to the early 20th century], Athens, Commercial Bank of Greece.

PICHOU, MYRSINI (2009), *Art and Women's Dress in England: The Classical Influence, circa 1789-1914*, MA history of art dissertation, London, Courtauld Institute of Art.

RIBEIRO, AILEEN (2003), *Dress and Morality*, Oxford/New York, Berg Publishers.

ROLLEY, KATRINA, and AISH, CAROLINE (in association with the National Portrait Gallery) (1992), *Fashion in Photographs, 1900-1920*, London, B. T. Batsford.

STERN, RADU (2004), *Against Fashion: Clothing as Art, 1850-1930*, Cambridge, MA, MIT Press.

Catalogue

SELECT BIBLIOGRAPHY

GÖRÜNÜR, LALE (2012), *Osmanli Imparatorluğu'nun son Döneminden Kadin Giysileri Sadberk Hanim Müzesi Koleksiyonu* [Women's costume of the late Ottoman era from the Sadberk Hanim Museum Collection], Istanbul, Sadberk Hanim Müzesi.

HATZIMICHALI, ANGELIKI (1925), *Ελληνική λαϊκή τέχνη. Σκύρος* [Greek folk art: Skyros], Athens.

— (1931), *Ελληνική λαϊκή τέχνη. Ρουμλούκι, Τρίκερι, Ικαρία* [Greek folk art: Roumlouki, Trikeri, Ikaria], Athens.

— (1948, 1954), *Ελληνικαί εθνικαί ενδυμασίαι* [Greek national costumes], illustrated by N. Sperling, vol. I: 1948, vol. II: 1954, Athens, Benaki Museum.

— (1978, 1983), *Η ελληνική λαϊκή φορεσιά* [The Greek folk costume], vol. I (1978): *Οι φορεσιές με το σιγκούνι* [Costumes with the *sigoúni*], vol. II (1983): *Οι φορεσιές με το καβάδι* [Costumes with the *kavádi*], Athens, Benaki Museum and Melissa Publishing House.

OIKONOMIDOU-YIANNARA, TATIANA (1966), «Η γυναικεία φορεσιά της Καρπάθου» [The women's costume of Karpathos], *Laographia: Bulletin of the Greek Folklore Society* XXIV: 254-267.

PAPANTONIOU, IOANNA (1976), «Οι χωρικές φορεσιές της Αργολιδοκορινθίας» [The village costumes of the Argolid and Corinthia], in *Πρακτικά Α' Διεθνούς Συνεδρίου Πελοποννησιακών Σπουδών* [Proceedings of the 1st international conference of Peloponnesian studies], vol. III, Sparta, 7-14 September 1975, Athens, Society for Peloponnesian Studies: 419-446.

— (1978), «Συμβολή στη μελέτη της γυναικείας ελληνικής παραδοσιακής φορεσιάς» [A contribution to the study of Greek women's traditional costumes], *Ethnographika* 1, Nafplio, Peloponnesian Folklore Foundation: 1-92.

— (1981), *Ελληνικές φορεσιές* [Greek costumes], Nafplio, Peloponnesian Folklore Foundation.

— (1996), *Ελληνικές τοπικές ενδυμασίες* [Greek regional costumes], Nafplio, Peloponnesian Folklore Foundation.

— (2000), *Η ελληνική ενδυμασία. Από την αρχαιότητα ως τις αρχές του 20ού αιώνα* [Greek costume: From antiquity to the early 20th century], Athens, Commercial Bank of Greece.

ZORA, POPI (1981), *Κεντήματα και κοσμήματα της ελληνικής φορεσιάς* [Embroideries and jewellery of Greek costumes], 2nd edn, Athens, Museum of Greek Folk Art, 1st edn 1966.

— (1994), *Λαϊκή τέχνη* [Folk art], Athens, Ekdotike Athenon.

Illustration Credits

CATALOGUE

© Peloponnesian Folklore Foundation, Nafplio: figs 2, 4 (2006.16.26), 5, 6, 8 (1998.16.4), 10 (2005.16.22), 11 (1976.16.8), 12, 13, 15, 16, 17, 18, 21, 23, 24, 25, 26 (1998.16.0041), 28 (2007.16.67), 29 (2007.16.66), 34 (2006.16.40), 37
© Alpha Bank Photographic Archive, Athens: figs 1, 3, 9, 33, 35
© Archbishop Makarios III Foundation, Cultural Center, Nicosia: fig. 36
© Benaki Museum, Athens: figs 7, 19 (ΓΕ 24101)
© Ethnological Museum (The House of Hadjigeorgakis Kornesios), Nicosia: fig. 27
© Lucy Braggiotti Editions, Athens: fig. 14
© National Gallery – Alexander Soutzos Museum, Athens: figs 20, 22 (K. 762)
© National Historical Museum, Athens: figs 30 (1483/44 α), 31 (1483/12 α)
© Society for the Promotion of Education and Learning [Philekpaideutiki Etaireia] Gallery, Athens: fig. 32

ESSAYS

Ioanna Papantoniou

© Acropolis Museum, Athens: fig. 3
© Hellenic Ministry of Culture and Sports / 21st Ephorate of Prehistoric and Classical Antiquities of the Cyclades: fig. 2
© Musée du Louvre, Paris: fig. 9
© Museum of Greek Folk Art, Athens: fig. 8 (A.M. 764)
© Peloponnesian Folklore Foundation, Nafplio: figs 1, 5, 6, 7, 11, 12, 13, 14

Angeliki Roumelioti

© Peloponnesian Folklore Foundation, Nafplio: figs 1, 2, 3, 4, 5, 6, 7, 8, 9, 10

Maria Passa-Kotsou

© Benaki Museum, Athens: figs 1 (29446), 2, 4 (29542), 10 (29451)
© Lyceum Club of Greek Women, Athens: figs 3, 5, 7, 8, 9
© Peloponnesian Folklore Foundation, Nafplio: fig. 6

Nadia Macha-Bizoumi

© Alpha Bank Photographic Archive, Athens: fig. 2
© Museum of the City of Athens – Vouros-Eutaxias Foundation, Athens: fig. 9 (243)
© Museum of the History of Greek Costume – Lyceum Club of Greek Women, Athens: figs 4 (14449), 5 (780), 8 (823)
© National Historical Museum, Athens: figs 3 (F-1B206), 7 (1483/12 α)
© Peloponnesian Folklore Foundation, Nafplio: figs 1, 6

Xenia Politou

© Benaki Museum, Athens: figs 3, 5, 7, 9
© National Historical Museum, Athens: fig. 1
© Peloponnesian Folklore Foundation, Nafplio: figs 4, 6, 8, 10
© State Russian Museum, St Petersburg: fig. 2

Sofia Pantouvaki

Photograph: Filep Motwary: fig. 1
© *Beyond Dress Codes: From Traditional Costume to Contemporary Fashion*, exhibition catalogue, Hellenic American Union, the Cyprus Fashion Designers Association and the Laiki Bank Cultural Centre, Nicosia 2012: fig. 3
© Dimitris Dassios Archive: fig. 2
© John Galliano Archives: figs 4a, 5a
© Municipal and Regional Theatre of Larissa Photographic Archive, Larissa: fig. 6
© Sofia Pantouvaki Collection: fig. 7
© Peloponnesian Folklore Foundation, Nafplio: figs 4b, 5b
© Takis Archive: fig. 8

Myrsini Pichou

© Birmingham Museums Trust: fig. 2 (1968M68)
© Gennadius Library – The American School of Classical Studies at Athens: fig. 1 (Volume I: 1842-1880)
© National Portrait Gallery, London: fig. 4 (whole-plate glass negative, NPG x33399)
© Peloponnesian Folklore Foundation, Nafplio: fig. 6 (2001.6.339)
© Victoria and Albert Museum, London, courtesy of Liberty's: fig. 3
© Victoria and Albert Museum, London: fig. 5

Biographical Notes

Ioanna Papantoniou

Stage and costume designer, Honorary Doctor of the Department of History and Archaeology, Aristotle University of Thessaloniki, Ioanna Papantoniou has worked with leading directors in state-run theatres and with independent companies. From 1956 to 1976 she was engaged in field research for costume studies. In 1974 she founded the Peloponnesian Folklore Foundation (1981 European Museum of the Year Main Award). In 1981 she was honoured by the Academy of Athens for services to scholarship and the theatre. She has taught in the Theatre Studies Departments of the Universities of Athens, Patras and the Peloponnese. In 2000 she was awarded the Gold Cross of the Order of the Phoenix by the President of Greece. In 2004 the Hellenic Centre for Theatrical Research awarded her the Panos Aravantinos Prize for her lifetime achievement in the theatre and in stage design. In 2013 she became the first winner of the Lifetime Achievement Award, newly instituted by the European Museum Academy (EMA).

Stamatis Zannos

He studied interior design and graphic arts at the Doxiadis School and Vakalo Art and Design College in Athens. Since 1980, he has been working as an interior architect and jewellery designer. In 1984, under the guidance of Ioanna Papantoniou, founder of the Peloponnesian Folklore Foundation, he started specialising in themed exhibitions and has since collaborated with numerous museums, foundations and other organisations, including the Peloponnesian Folklore Foundation, the Benaki Museum, the Greek Ministry of Culture, the Museum of Greek Folk Art, the National Technical University of Athens, the National Hellenic Research Foundation, the Study Centre for Contemporary Ceramics, the Ephorate of Underwater Antiquities, the Foundation of the Hellenic World, Alpha Bank, the Hellenic Centre London, the Alexander Fleming Foundation, the Goulandris Natural History Museum – Gaia Centre, the Hellenic Parliament Foundation, the Museum of Cycladic Art, the Teloglion Foundation of Art, the Museum of Contemporary Art in Thessaloniki and the Numismatic Museum.

Nadia Macha-Bizoumi

She studied history and archaeology at the University of Ioannina. In 2011 she was awarded a doctorate in folklore studies (with an emphasis on clothing) from the Department of History and Ethnology of the Democritus University of Thrace. In 2006 she completed a course in museum science (Hellenic American Educational Foundation, specialised course in museum science and cultural management). She has taken part in research projects relating to the recording, documenting and digitising of museum-type costume collections and has curated numerous costume exhibitions. She is a founder member and Vice-President of the Hellenic Costume Society and a member of the International Council of Museums (ICOM), the ICOM Costume Committee (ICC) and the Greek Folklore Society.

Sofia Pantouvaki

A professor of costume design in the Department of Film, TV and Scenography at Aalto University in Finland, she has a doctorate in scenography from the Central Saint Martins College of Arts and Design, London, and she specialised in scenography and costume design for opera and ballet at La Scala, Milan. Her design credits include more than 70 theatrical, operatic and dance productions in Greece and elsewhere, and she won the awards for best production design and best costumes at the Drama [northern Greece] Short Film Festival

(2005). She has curated and designed numerous exhibitions. She is a member of the global editorial board of the magazine *Catwalk: The Journal of Fashion, Beauty and Style*; an editor of the journal *Studies in Costume and Performance* (Intellect, 2015), co-author of *A History of Dress: The Western World and Greece* [in Greek] (2010), editor of *Giannis Metsis: Athens Experimental Ballet* [in Greek] (2011) and co-editor of *Presence and Absence: The Performing Body* (forthcoming). She was a judge and curator of costume design at the *World Stage Design 2013* exhibition.

Maria Papadopoulou
Born in Thessaloniki, she is a graduate of the Department of International and European Studies at the Panteion University, Athens, and has attended seminars on advertising and marketing, media studies, radio, and information technology. She worked in the field of advertising and marketing from 1977 to 1988 and is a former advertising manager of the Argolida FM radio station. She has been editor-in-chief of the magazines *Deka* and *Nyfi* and public relations manager of TORA-TORA Mail. She has edited numerous collections of documents, periodicals and books. Since 1996 she has been working at the Peloponnesian Folklore Foundation as head of the Department for Digital Documentation of the Museum Collections and coordinator of the Foundation's publications and periodic exhibitions. She was a member of the team formed to digitise museum exhibits and upload them to the Digital Library of the European TEXMEDIN project and is a participant in the Europeana Fashion project.

Maria Passa-Kotsou
Born in Athens in 1955, she studied at Athens University (Department of History and Archaeology) with a state scholarship. Concurrently, she attended the School of Tourist Guides and has worked as a qualified tourist guide for 35 years. From 1981 to 1985 she worked as a research assistant at the Peloponnesian Folklore Foundation, studying and indexing travellers' writings for the compilation of an archive relating to Greek costumes, and editing the catalogue of exhibits in the PFF Museum in Nafplio. She also indexed the issues of the *Athenische Mitteilungen* as an external staff member of Ioannina University. Her starting point for this academic work, and a foundation of practical experience, was her membership of the Lyceum Club of Greek Women dance company in Athens (1972-2002), which made her familiar with the principles of traditional Greek costumes. Since 1988, she has worked as a volunteer for the Lyceum's Museum of the History of Greek Costume on the organisation of exhibitions, the presentation of dress shows and the recording of traditional customs. She is currently 1st Vice-President of the Board of the Lyceum Club of Greek Women.

Myrsini Pichou
Born in Athens, she works in the Athens University History Museum. She has a postgraduate degree in cultural organisations management from the Hellenic Open University and completed her postgraduate studies under Professor Aileen Ribeiro at the Courtauld Institute of Art in London. In 2004 she assisted the artistic director Vassilis Zidianakis with the planning of the exhibition *Ptychoseis = Folds + Pleats: Drapery from Ancient Greek Dress to 21st Century Fashion*, organised by the Peloponnesian Folklore Foundation. She collaborated with ATOPOS Contemporary Visual Culture to organise the *RRRIPP!! Paper Fashion* dress exhibition. She is a member of the board of the Hellenic Costume Society and Co-Chair of the Greek Alumni Group of the Courtauld Institute of Art. She is also a member of the Lyceum Club of Greek Women, the Costume Society, the Association of Dress Historians and the International Council of Museums Costume Committee.

Xenia Politou
She was born in Athens and read French and comparative philology in Athens and Paris. From 1993 to 2001, she worked at the Museum of the History of Greek Costume, Athens. At the same time she also assisted

with the National Archive of Greek Traditional Costume, a research programme on clothing subsidised by the Greek Ministry of Culture. Between 2002 and 2005, she worked for the Peloponnesian Folklore Foundation on the organisation of the *Ptychoseis = Folds + Pleats: Drapery from Ancient Greek Dress to 21st Century Fashion* exhibition, the first international fashion exhibition in Greece. Since March 2005, she has been working at the Benaki Museum, and since September 2010 she has been Curator of its Neohellenic Culture Collection. Her research interests include the study of Greek local costumes and the formation of museum collections of costumes. She is a founder member and Secretary of the Hellenic Costume Society.

Angeliki Roumelioti

She is responsible for the collections of the Peloponnesian Folklore Foundation, where she has been working since 1992 under the supervision of Ioanna Papantoniou. She has coordinated and curated numerous PFF periodic exhibitions in Greece and abroad; and she has collaborated with some of the established experts in the field of costume in documenting the Foundation's collections. Since 2008, she has participated in a research project on the subject of Nafplio dressmakers, initiated by the Hellenic Costume Society, the first results of which were presented at one of the Society's seminars. She took part in the European TEXMEDIN project and is a member of the team working on the current Europeana Fashion project. She is a member of the International Council of Museums (ICOM) and a founder member of the Hellenic Costume Society.

A

Abito: a woman's skirt (Corfu)

Aéras: tulle headscarf (Skopelos)

Aladzás: a multicoloured striped or chequered cotton material (Turk. *alaca*)

Alum: a double sulphate of aluminium and potassium that fixes the dyes used for the yarns

Ambediá: bodice of the sleeved dress; also, the shoulder straps of the *koutsomániko* dress (q.v.) (Astypalaia)

Ambrákami (pl.): type of necklace (Karpathos)

Ampechone: ancient Greek outer garment made of a shaggy woollen fabric, worn by women and some effeminate young men

Ampechonion: a smaller and lighter version of the ampechonon

Ampechonon: kind of outer garment of moderate size • a military garment

Anderí: a sort of coat dress (the Levant) • bridal coat (Stefanoviki, Roumlouki, Ioannina) • a sleeved ankle-length garment worn by priests under the *ráso* (cassock)

Anetoráli: a very short white silk chemise (Skopelos)

Antitsémbera (pl.): supplementary kerchiefs (Karpathos)

Arkélia (pl.): seaweed yielding a dark red or crimson dye (Trikeri)

Arkiláto: dark red silk chemise (Trikeri)

Arvanítika (pl.): a rural type of women's costume (Attica)

Asiménia: a yellow *bólia* (q.v.) (Astypalaia)

Áspri vólta: a long, sleeveless, pleated overdress (Skopelos)

B

Bambazína: a long silk scarf, or the costume with which it is worn (Mesta)

Bambouklí: a very short, long-sleeved jacket (Skopelos)

Bibíla or **pipíla**: a kind of fine white needlepoint lace (Cyprus)

Bibizári: a silk fabric

Bólia: a long silk or cotton scarf forming part of the headdress (Corinthia, Argolid, Attica, Corfu, Euboea, Psara, Skyros)

Bólka: see *polka*

Bougasía: red lining (Episkopi)

Boumbári: a component of the headdress (Corfu)

Bounés: a component of the headdress made of black bouclé wool (Skopelos)

Boustína: dickey (Corfu)

Braccae, -arum, or **bracae**: white breeches, originally Celtic, pleated at the waist

Broumánika: the separate sleeves of the bridal costume (Roumlouki) • the sleeves of the *bambouklí* (q.v.) (Skopelos)

C

Chlaina: an ancient Roman dark-coloured cloak, which in winter was also used as a coverlet • a thick garment fastened with a fibula

Chlamys: a men's short cloak fastened with a clasp on the right shoulder

Chrysés vétses (pl.): red stockings trimmed with gold braid (Astypalaia)

Chrysí: the bridal and festive costume (Skyros)

Chrysí fellí (pl.): gold-embroidered mules (Astypalaia)

Chrysokap'tséli: see *kapitsáli* (Skopelos)

Chrysokímero: gold-embroidered belt (Corfu)

Chrysokóndosso: a gold-embroidered black felt jacket (Karpathos)

Chrysomándilo: a pearl-encrusted frontlet; also the entire costume incorporating it (Astypalaia)

Chrysós sákos: see *kavádi* (Kastelorizo)

Chrysosklavariká: embroidery done with gold wire

Chrysóspastos: gold-embroidered, made of cloth-of-gold (Byzantium)

Chrysózoni: see *chrysokímero*

Clavi (pl.): decorative bands on Roman garments

D

Dalmatic: a sleeved garment of the Early Christian period that perhaps originated in Dalmatia, a variant of the *tunica* (q.v.); it is made up from more than one piece of cloth sewn together, with or without sleeves

Damató: silk chemise (Kymi)

Devitísia (pl.): a Byzantine fabric

Diplári: an almost square, gold-embroidered apron (Episkopi)

Doúla foustáni: a glossy, black, sleeveless, pleated dress (Kymi)

Doulamás: a long brocade outer garment (Sifnos, Ios) • a woman's sleeveless outer garment (*pirpirí*, q.v.) of dark felt with *terzídika* (q.v.) embroidery in gold and dark colours (Ioannina)

Dzákos: a short bodice with short sleeves: a sort of *zipoúni* (q.v.) (Attica, Corinthia, Argolid)

Dzipoúni: a type of sleeveless waistcoat (Sifnos, Ios)

Dzouloúfia (pl.): loose strands of hair forming curls (Skopelos, Pyrgi)

Dzoumbés: a sleeved or sleeveless coat dress of Ottoman origin, often fur-lined

E

Embliá or **embleá**: the pleated skirt of the dress (Astypalaia)

Emboliá asiméni: the inner *bólia* (q.v.) of the *chrysomándilo* (q.v.) headdress (Astypalaia)

Exomis: a short woollen chiton leaving one shoulder uncovered, worn by Spartan women and peasants from the late 6th century BC onwards

F

Fanéla: an undergarment (Episkopi)

Fascia (pl.): criss-cross thongs to protect the legs (ancient Rome)

Fengári: a large red 'moon' adorning the kerchief (Kymi)

Feredzés: a type of outer garment of Ottoman origin with an exceptionally large collar which was worn over the head

Férmeli: a waistcoat left unbuttoned, worn with the foustanella

Fidáto: a name for the *kavádi* (q.v.), from the sinuous design on the material (Kastelorizo)

Fioúmbes (pl.): silver or silver-gilt links like cufflinks (Corfu)

Foúndes (pl.): linen or woollen tassels on the hem and sleeves of the chemise (Thessaly) • silk tassels on the *katsoúli* (q.v.) (Roumlouki)

Foúndi: a sleeveless chemise with embroidered hem (Attica)

Foustána or **f'stána**: a pleated sleeveless dress (Skopelos) (see also *stófa*)

Foúta: apron (Roumlouki)

F'tas: a large silk and cotton kerchief (Skyros)

G

Gázi, gándzi (pl.): jewelled ornaments (Karpathos)

G'dóres (pl.): type of backless shoes or slippers (Skyros)

Geránio: blue linen chemise with multicoloured embroideries

Gólfia (pl.): jewelled ornaments (Karpathos)

Goúna: sleeveless waistcoat (Skyros) • gold-embroidered velvet outer garment (Kastelorizo) • a short velvet or satin jacket worn over the *koutsomániko* (q.v.) (Astypalaia)

Gounéla: a type of woman's waistcoat (Kymi)

Graftá (pl.): embroideries for which the designs are drawn freehand on the cloth and embroidered without counting, usually with the aid of a frame

Granátsa or **granátza**: a very long-sleeved Byzantine outer garment of Asiatic origin

Gríza (pl. **gríza**) or **grízo** or **grízo me ta chrysá**: a white, medium-length, sleeveless felt coat (Attica)

Gýros: part of the headdress (Karpathos)

H

Haimalí: silver amulet • a jewelled ornament (Stefanoviki)

Hanáka: chain necklace (Athens)

Helkechitones (pl.): those who wore long chitons

Heráki: a special brooch holding the kerchief in place (Saronic Islands)

Herákia (pl.): jewelled ornaments (Karpathos)

Himation: a large rectangle of woollen material that was wrapped round the body

Histos: warp-weighted vertical loom

I

Ílios: a jewelled ornament (Corfu)

K

Kafássi: home-made decorative frontlet (Stefanoviki)

Kaftan: a luxury sleeved outer garment, often fur-lined • a long luxurious robe worn by men in the Middle East • an open-fronted, sleeved garment (Soufli)

Káïsma: the process of treating cotton warp thread in a mash of flour

Kaliaráto: a type of chemise whose sleeves are embroidered all over with motifs resembling *kaliáres* (cockroaches) (Astypalaia)

Kalpáki: kalpak, a type of round cap worn by women

Káltsa tou vrakioú: the lower ends of the *vráka* (q.v.), made of a separate piece of luxury fabric (Kastelorizo)

Kambánes (pl.): jewelled ornaments (Karpathos, Corfu)

Kanalotí: a type of skirt (Sifnos, Ios)

Kap'hás: sleeveless pleated dress (Skyros)

Kapitsáli: the chinstrap of the headdress (Salamis, Kymi, Skopelos)

Kaplamás: a sleeved outer garment

Karkavelónes (pl.): headdress ornaments (Mesta)

Kaskí: see *tsakí*

Katifés: sleeveless velvet outer garment (Stefanoviki)

Katománika (pl.): embroidered separate sleeves of the *dzákos* (q.v.) (Boeotia, Attica)

Katsoúli: the basis or the whole of the headdress (Roumlouki)

Kavádi: a type of sleeveless outer garment (Kastelorizo) • a dress of rich brocade (Peloponnese, Athens, etc.)

Kavadománika (pl.): oversleeves of the Karagouna costume (Thessaly)

Kavá'i: a type of sleeved dress; also, the whole female costume (Elymbos [Karpathos])

Kavoúki: a very small round cap (Skopelos)

Kenéziko: silk shawl from China (Kastelorizo)

Kinária (pl.): stripes on the selvages

Kioustéki: silver chain (Crete) • a type of chain ornament (Stefanoviki)

Klidotária (pl.): large silver buckles (Trikeri, Sarakatsani)

Klóni (pl.): jewelled ornaments (Karpathos)

Kofináki: a special pin to secure the headdress (Saronic Islands)

Kolaína: a gold-embroidered dickey (Skopelos)

Kolonáto: a chemise with embroidery arranged in columns (Peloponnese)

Kolovóli: an underdress or petticoat like a crinoline, reinforced on the inside with hoops to distend the skirt (Skopelos) • petticoat (Trikeri, Skyros) • sleeveless pleated underdress

Kolpos: overfold or overfall

Kombovelónes (pl.): special pins to secure the *chrysomándilo* (q.v.) (Astypalaia)

Kondándero: a sort of short coat dress (Stefanoviki)

Kondogoúni: sleeved velvet waistcoat (the 'Amalia')

Kondóssi: a kind of waistcoat (Roumlouki)

Kondoúres (pl.): slippers (Skopelos)

Kondovrátsi: a silk *vráka* (q.v.) (Kastelorizo)

Koróna: the middle section of the articulated belt, decorated with enamel and filigree; also the whole belt (Thrace) • a home-made bridal headdress (Attica)

Koronátsi or **xelítsi**: an ornamental gold frontlet (Attica)

Korvéti: a large decorative motif on the hem of the bridal chemise (Trikeri)

Kósses (pl.): silver ornaments for the plaits (Trikeri)

Kouloúra: the basis of the headdress (Astypalaia)

Koumbouféles (pl.): pins to secure the kerchief (Episkopi)

Kouroúkla: print kerchief (Cyprus)

Koutelítis: headdress ornament (Karpathos)

Koutsomániko: a sleeveless silk or satin dress with shoulder straps (Astypalaia)

Kremasídi: a pendant (Astypalaia)

Kremastária or **piskoúlia** (pl.): ornaments enlaced in the plaits (Peloponnese)

Krémezo: red velvet jacket (Corfu)
Kremizí: the medium red dye used for chemises, which comes from the kermes, a parasite found on trees (Trikeri)
Krépi: silk shawl worn on the head (Kastelorizo)

L
Lahoúri: multicoloured woollen kerchief (Karpathos)
Langhióli or **ladzoúli** or **lóxa** or **loxári** or **klínghia**: a triangular piece of material; a number of these (scalene right-angled triangles) make up the foustanella
Lapatsás: a very long-sleeved Byzantine outer garment of Asiatic origin
Linomániko: a Karagouna's chemise
Loros or **lorus**: a sash wrapped round the body in a deacon's vestments
Louloudáto: a name for the *kavádi* (q.v.), from the flowered design of the material (Kastelorizo)
Lóxa: see *langhióli*

M
Mag'líka: a headscarf forming part of the headdress (Soufli)
Maístra: a specialist embroideress responsible for the embroideries on the hem of the bridal chemise (Attica)
Malakófi: hooped petticoat (Skopelos)
Mallína: a kind of woollen petticoat (Trikeri)
Mallítiko: woollen kerchief (Karpathos)
Mána: the central front part of various women's and men's garments
Mandíli tou kórfou: a costly kerchief (Trikeri)
Margaritarénia skoúfia: a cap with the front embroidered all over with gold and pearls (Astypalaia)
Márka: a brooch with the wearer's name, holding the kerchief in place (Saronic Islands)
Maschalister: a continuous band to hold ancient Greek garments in place, which was crossed over at the back and passed under the armpits
Masoúr' plexídes (pl.): silver ornaments worn in the plaits (Attica)
Mastrapás: a spouted brass jug with a lid • the motif embroidered on the bridal chemise (Attica)
Mendenés: a waistcoat of patterned brocade (Skyros)
Mesofoústano: petticoat (Sifnos, Ios)
Messáli: see *bólia* (Argolid and Corinthia)
Mórkos: richly pleated sleeveless dress (Skopelos)
Myrimídia (pl.):a necklace (Karpathos)

O
Olóskepo: see *sképi*
Ombólia: same as *bólia*
Ópsi: the central section of the *bólia* (q.v.) (Skyros)
Ordalíki: see *yordalíki*
Ouyióto or **ouvyiotó** or **ouvyiastó** or **kinnarotó** or **lourotó**: a textile with woven-in stripes made of a different yarn from the rest of the cloth, i.e. gold thread, cotton, thicker silk or boiled silk

P
Panomoustouchiá: a *bólia* (q.v.) with embroidered ends (Astypalaia)
Paoúnia (pl.): special silver head ornaments (Soufli)
Papázi or **papáz'**: the central stem of the tassel of a fez; also, the flat round woman's cap of the 'Amalia'
Passamádes: the gold embroidery on the *pesselí* (q.v.) (Corfu)
Pekámiso: the bridal chemise (Kastelorizo)
Peloúzi: a velvety material (plush or velours)
Peplos: an ancient Greek woman's garment made of a single piece of material, fastened with two pins at the shoulders
Peristéra: a white kerchief forming part of the headdress (Roumlouki)
Pesselí: gold-embroidered woman's jacket (Corfu)
Pétsa: silk kerchief (Sifnos, Ios)
Phainomeris: an ancient Greek short woollen peplos (q.v.) resembling the *exomis* (q.v.) but open on one side, worn by Spartan women

Pharos: an ancient Greek scarf-like outer garment
Phelonion: a priestly vestment of the Orthodox Church
Piétes (pl.): type of headscarf (Saronic Islands)
Pína: a distinctive inner cap (Sifnos, Ios)
Pipíla (pl. **pipíles**): see *bibíla*
Pirpirí: a kind of sleeveless outer garment, gold-embroidered; a variant of the *doulamás* (q.v.) (Epiros)
Piskoúlia: see *kremastária*
Pitsília (pl.): beaded lace trimming of the kerchief (Karpathos)
Podemí: footwear (shoes and stockings) (Skyros)
Podiés (pl.): the gold-embroidered panels on the inside of the lower front corners of the skirt of the *sayás* (q.v.) (Roumlouki, Asvestohori, Pylaia)
Podonári or **podanári**: trouser legs • the lower ends of the *vráka* (q.v.)
Póli: the decorated inside faces of the *sayás* (q.v.) (Episkopi)
Polka or **polkaki** or **bólka**: a woman's sleeved jacket that buttons over the bust and covers the upper part of the skirt
Pórpi: a wide silver belt (Stefanoviki)
Poukámiso me ta chrysá: gold-embroidered sleeved chemise (Skyros)
Poukámiso me ta sarídia: bridal chemise (Drymos)
Poýdere: hem (Kynouria, Skyros)

R
Ramónes (pl.): a special manner of dressing a Karagouna's hair (Thessaly)
Raxíni: small red cap (Kastelorizo)
Reed: part of the loom consisting of a closely spaced row of thin reeds attached to a wooden frame
Repunta: backstitch (Karpathos)
Rokéto: petticoat (Corfu)

S
Sagum, **-i**: a thick cloak worn by Roman soldiers
Sakofoústano or **sákos**: skirt and *polka* (q.v.) (Karpathos)
Salivária (pl.) or **salvári**: men's or women's wide trousers like the *vráka* (q.v.), of Oriental origin
Sálpa: a headdress ornament (Skopelos)
Samaráki: a short dress (Mesta)
Sárka: sleeved or sleeveless jacket (Cyprus)
Satakroúta (**seta cruda**): a silk fabric used for skirts (Cyprus)
Sayás: sleeved, open-fronted cotton coat dress (Roumlouki, Asvestohori, Pylaia, Episkopi, Karagouna)
Segmentum, **-i**: a purple or other decorative motif on Roman and Early Christian garments
Serái kapáki: a particular shape for the ends of the sleeves
Shaft: a component of the loom consisting of a bunch of thick yarns attached to two wooden bars; it is moved by the treadles to raise and lower the warp threads alternately
Sigoúni or **segoúni** or **sigoúna** or **segoúna**: a sleeveless woollen outer garment worn mainly in Central Greece, the Peloponnese and elsewhere
Skaramángio: a luxury fabric in various colours • a sleeved chiton made of *skaramángio*, worn by Byzantine emperors, courtiers and other nobles
Sképi or **olóskepo**: a fine silk fabric in various colours used to make the chemises for formal wear (Trikeri)
Skléta (pl.): type of festive costume (Astypalaia)
Skolarítsia (pl.): earrings (Karpathos)
Skolopendráto: a type of chemise, the sleeves of which are embroidered all over with motifs resembling scolopendras (centipedes) (Astypalaia)
Skoúta: the skirt of the chemise (Skyros) • the embroidered border of the *sayás* (q.v.) (Macedonia)
Souyiás: a type of ornament (Stefanoviki)
Spanióliko: a type of silk shawl (Kastelorizo)
Spíles (pl.): gold brooches (Corfu)
Sprang: a special kind of mesh used for belts
Staftádes (pl.): the red ribbons of the headdress (Corfu)

Stithópano: breast kerchief (Mesta)

Stófa: brocade • a sleeveless pleated dress (Skopelos); see also *foustána* (q.v.)

Stola: an outer garment similar to the himation (q.v.), worn by the ancient Romans

Stólos: the bridal and festive headdress (Corfu)

Stroudáto: the name of a type of *kavádi* (q.v.), from the 'oyster' shape of the decorative design (Kastelorizo)

Syrmakésiko: couched embroidery with gold or silver thread

T

Tabula: a large square Roman decorative motif sewn on to the tunic, either purple or gold-embroidered or made of costly brocade

Tambári: a very long-sleeved outer garment; see also *tzitzákia* (q.v.)

Taraklí: a striped material with a specially dyed warp (Stefanoviki, Episkopi)

Tarapoulούz: a sash round the hips (Kastelorizo)

Terlíkia or **terlítsia** (pl.): women's closed shoes, either knitted or made of cloth (Skyros)

Terzídiko: couching embroidery, a technique which involves forming the design by laying gold thread or silk or woollen twist on the outer surface of the cloth and holding it in place with fine stitches

Terzís or **terzías**: a tailor specialising in the sewing and embroidering of outer garments

Thilykotária (pl.): silver belt buckles (Kymi)

Thymiatí: an apron with specially woven decorative designs, the *thymiatá* (Soufli)

Timbadóxa (pl.): interior sleeve ornamentation (Skopelos)

Tir-tir: twisted strips of gold or gilt metal

Toga: cloak

Tokás: a small round hook

Torkós: a headdress formed of four black *boumbária* (q.v.) with red ribbons (Corfu)

Trákma: gold-embroidered frontlet (Episkopi)

Trémouses (pl.): spangles (Skopelos)

Tribon: a thick woollen chiton worn by ancient Spartan men

Tsakí or **kaskí**: a crown-like band of material worn round the *raxíni* (q.v.) (Kastelorizo)

Tsatsaráki: a decorative ribbon on the *kolaína* (q.v.) (Skopelos)

Tsembéri or **tsembéra**: a type of kerchief (Saronic Islands, Attica, Episkopi)

Tsiboukotó: a type of off-white pure silk chemise (Psara)

Tsipfí: a kind of waistcoat (Sifnos, Ios)

Tsitsákia (pl.): long gold strings embellished with *tir-tir* (q.v.) and spangles, terminating in a stylised flower made of the same materials and pearls; a headdress accessory (Skopelos)

Tsoúla: a triangular metal ornament worn on the back (Astypalaia)

Tsourápia (pl.): knitted white stockings with toes and heels of a different colour (Episkopi)

Tunica: Roman tunic

Tzitzákio: a type of military cloak similar to the *tambári* (q.v.) (It. *tabarro*) • a thick outer garment or cloak of the Byzantines

V

Vathráki: a rectangular piece of material inserted in the armpit to make it easier to attach the sleeve

Veléssi: a woman's skirt (Corfu)

Velonáki: an ornament (Trikeri)

Veloúdo: the sleeved dress of the *chrysomándilo* (q.v.), made of velvet (Astypalaia)

Vérges (pl.): earrings (Corfu, Astypalaia)

Vétses (pl.): broad bands of embroidery on the *skolopendráto* (q.v.) chemise (Astypalaia)

Voúkles (pl.): gold clasps fastening the neck opening of the chemise (Kastelorizo)

Vouklí: a cord sewn on to the inside of the sleeve of the chemise (Astypalaia)

Vráka: baggy bloomers • pleated knee-length or ankle-length breeches • the main garment of the men's or women's costume, or the whole costume, in the Greek Islands and Asia Minor

Vrakozóni, -óna: a drawstring round the leg of the *vráka* (q.v.) (Kastelorizo) • a woman's embroidered girdle round the waist of the *vráka* (q.v.)

W

Warp: the threads stretched out lengthwise in a loom to be crossed by the weft
Weft or **woof**: yarn that is threaded by the shuttle through the warp threads on the loom; collectively, all the threads of the cloth running at right angles to the selvage

X

Xelítsi: see *koronátsi*
Xombliastá (pl.): drawn embroidery, where by counting the stitches the embroiderer can create repeated patterns

Y

Yiádema: headdress (Corfu)
Yialabí: sleeved velvet jacket (Kymi)
Yiléki: the embroidered short sleeveless waistcoat of the Karagouna • the inner sleeveless waistcoat of the foustanella costume • a type of sleeveless men's waistcoat (Ioannina, Corfu, Crete, Cyprus)
Yiminiá or **yemeniá** (pl.): type of slippers (Karpathos, Mesta) (Ar. *yamani*)
Yordalíki or **ordalíki**: a jewelled ornament (Karpathos)
Yoúrda: woman's sleeveless coat with embroidery in dark wool (Kifissia [Attica])

Z

Zatoúni: a gathered, sleeved silk dress (Astypalaia)
Zepoúni: a silk jacket (Kastelorizo)
Zipoúni: a kind of jacket (Cyprus, Saronic Islands) • sleeveless waistcoat (Corfu)
Zonári: waist ornament (Astypalaia) • a gold-embroidered belt (Stefanoviki)
Zosiés (pl.): chain-link belt (Astypalaia)
Zósma: belt (Kastelorizo)
Zostíra: a ribbon attached to the headdress (Sifnos, Ios)
Zóstra: a belt of a special kind of mesh (Corinthia, Argolida)

Index

Note: Page numbers with an asterisk refer to illustrations.

The book

Patterns of Magnificence
TRADITION AND REINVENTION IN GREEK WOMEN'S COSTUME

edited by Ioanna Papantoniou

was printed in Athens in January 2014

in 1000 copies in English
and 1000 copies in Greek.

It was produced by PEAK PUBLISHING
and printed by BAXAS S.A.

for the Hellenic Centre, London.